COMMITTEE FOR
TECHNICAL EDUCATION

A J Barker

Pearl Harbor

Editor-in-Chief: Barrie Pitt
Art Director: Peter Dunbar

Military Consultant: Sir Basil Liddell Hart
Picture Editor: Bobby Hunt

Executive Editor: David Mason
Art Editor: Sarah Kingham
Designer: John Marsh
Cover: Denis Piper
Research Assistant: Yvonne Marsh
Cartographer: Richard Natkiel
Special Drawings: John Batchelor

Contents

The fatal flaw

Introduction by Captain Sir Basil Liddell Hart

From 1931 onward the Japanese were aggressively engaged in expanding their footholds on the Asiatic mainland at the expense of the Chinese, who were weakened by internal conflict, and to the detriment of American and British interests in that sphere. In that year they had invaded Manchuria and converted it into a Japanese satellite state. Following Hitler's conquest of France and the Low Countries in 1940, the Japanese took advantage of France's helplessness by getting her to agree, under threat, to their 'protective' occupation of French Indo-China.

In reply President Roosevelt demanded, on the 24th July 1941, the withdrawal of Japanese troops from Indo-China – and to enforce his demand he issued orders on the 26th for freezing all Japanese assets in the USA and placing an embargo on oil supply. Mr. Churchill took simultaneous action, and two days later the refugee Dutch Government in London was induced to follow suit – which meant, as Mr. Churchill had remarked, that 'Japan was deprived

at a stroke of her vital oil supplies.'

In earlier discussions, as far back as 1931, it had always been recognized that such a paralysing stroke would force Japan to fight, as the only alternative to collapse or the abandonment of her policy. It is remarkable that she deferred striking for more than four months, while trying to negotiate a lifting of the oil embargo. The United States Government refused to lift it, unless Japan withdrew not only from Indo-China but also from China. No Government, least of all the Japanese, could be expected to swallow such humiliating conditions, and utter loss of face. So there was ample reason to expect war in the Pacific at any moment, from the last week of July onwards. In these circumstances the Americans and British were lucky to be allowed four months' grace before the Japanese struck. But little advantage was taken of this interval for defensive preparation.

On 7th December 1941, a Japanese naval force with six aircraft carriers delivered a shattering air attack on Pearl Harbor, the American naval base in the Hawaiian Islands. The stroke was made ahead of the declaration of war, following the precedent of that on Port Arthur in 1904, Japan's opening stroke in her war against Russia.

Until early in 1941 Japan's plan in case of war against the United States was to use her main fleet in the southern Pacific in conjunction with an attack on the Philippine Islands, to meet an American advance across the ocean to the relief of their garrison in the Philippines. That was the move that the Americans were expecting the Japanese to make.

Admiral Yamamoto, however, had in the meantime conceived a new plan – of a surprise attack on Pearl Harbor. The striking force made a roundabout approach via the Kurile Islands and came down from the north upon the Hawaiian Islands undetected, then launching its attack before sunrise, with 360 aircraft, from a position nearly 300 miles from Pearl Harbor.

Thereby the way was cleared for an uninterrupted seaborne invasion of American, British and Dutch territories in that Ocean. While the main Japanese striking force had been steaming north-east towards the Hawaiian Islands, other naval forces had been escorting troopship convoys into the South-west Pacific.

At Pearl Harbor the targets, in order of importance, were: the US carriers (it was hoped by the Japanese that as many as six, and at least three, would be at Pearl Harbor); the US battleships; the oil-tanks and other port installations; the aircraft on the main bases at Wheeler, Hickam and Bellows Field.

The main task force assembled on 22nd November at Tankan Bay in the Kurile Islands, and left on the 26th. On 2nd December it received word that the attack orders were confirmed, so ships were darkened; even then there was the proviso that the mission would be abandoned if the fleet was spotted before 6th December or if a last-minute settlement was reached in Washington.

There was disappointment when on the 6th, the eve of the stroke, no US carriers were reported in Pearl Harbor. (Actually one was on the Californian Coast, another taking bombers to Midway, and another had just delivered fighters to Wake, while three were in the Atlantic). However, eight battleships were reported to be in Pearl Harbor, and without torpedo nets, so Admiral Nagumo decided to go ahead. The aircraft were launched between 0600 and 0715 hours (Hawaii time) next morning, about 275 miles due north of Pearl Harbor.

The attack started at 0755 and went on until 0825; then a second wave, of dive-bombers and high-level bombers, struck at 0840. But the use of the torpedo-bombers in the first wave had been the decisive factor. Of the American battleships, five were sunk and the other three were severely damaged. Of the American aircraft, 188 were destroyed, and sixty-three damaged. The Japanese loss was only twenty-nine planes destroyed and seventy damaged – apart from the five midget submarines which were lost in an attack that was a complete failure. Of human casualties, the USA had 3,435 killed or wounded; while the Japanese figure is more uncertain, the killed were under 100. The returning Japanese aircraft landed on the carriers between 1030 and 1330 hours. On 23rd December the main task force itself arrived back in Japan.

The coup brought three great advantages to Japan. The US Pacific Fleet was completely put out of action. The operations in the South-west Pacific were made secure against naval interference, while the Pearl Harbor task force could now be employed to support the latter operations. The Japanese were now allowed more time to extend and build up their defensive ring.

The fatal flaw was that the stroke had missed the US carriers – its prime target, and had also missed the oil tanks and other important installations, whose destruction would have made the American recovery much slower, as Pearl Harbor was the only full fleet base. Coming as a surprise, apparently before any declaration of war, it aroused such indignation in America as to unit public opinion behind President Roosevelt, and in violent anger against Japan.

Prelude

During the 16th Century Shogun Hideyoshi brought peace and unity to a Japan that had been racked by civil war for over a hundred years. Having made himself supreme in Japan, Hideyoshi then looked for other worlds to conquer, and Korea seemed a natural stepping-stone to the conquest of China. Thus it was that in 1592, after Korea had declined to permit the passage of Japanese troops through the peninsular for an attack on China, the first of Hideyoshi's two invasions of Korea was launched. The Japanese armies drove all before them and were soon masters of the country. But Hideyoshi had failed to ensure the safety of his sea communication, and a squadron of primitive iron-clad Korean warships sank his fleet, severed his army's supply line and forced its withdrawal. This made Hideyoshi appreciate the necessity of controlling the sea and, when a second invasion was attempted, his plan was almost the same as that used at Pearl Harbor three and a half centuries later. While Japanese diplomats were still talking in Seoul, Hideyoshi attacked without warning.

The defending ships were destroyed and the Japanese troops landed. But this time the Chinese were fighting beside the Koreans and the Japanese armies met with desperate resistance. Eventually they were forced back, compelled to withdraw, and annihilated when they tried to sail back to Japan. For the second time the Japanese had learned that the success of an overseas campaign depended not only on the quality of the land forces employed but also on command of the seas. On his deathbed the defeated Hideyoshi is said to have expressed regret that he should have caused the death of so many of his fellow countrymen in foreign lands, and issued his famous edict of isolation. As a result the Japanese were cut off from the rest of the world for over 200 years.

The long era of seclusion came to an end in July 1853 when a squadron of American warships sailed uninvited into Tokyo Bay, and the occasion is recorded in Japanese annals as 'The Day of the Black Ships'. Impressed by the multitude and magnitude of the guns bristling from the sides of the American ships and by the vessels which belched black smoke and moved independently of sail and wind, the Japanese warlords saw the need for guns and ships. This American exercise in gunboat diplomacy brought about the end of Japan's feudal heritage, and led to her modernisation and westernisation as well as the acquisition of her own 'black ships'. By 1897 the Japanese were ordering and building warships faster than any other country except Britain, and by the turn of the century Japan's Imperial Navy was as big and modern as that of many Western powers. To man it went the cream of Japanese youth

Almost exactly three centuries after Hideyoshi's defeat, Japan decided on another invasion of the Chinese mainland. Russian influence had been growing in Korea, where Japan's commercial interests were all important. Also, in 1898 Russia had acquired the Manchurian fortress of Port Arthur and the intention to link it by rail to Europe for the transportation of troops and supplies was seen as a threat to Japan's very existence as an independent state. By the close of the 19th Century the Japanese press was already talking of war with the Colossus of the West and Japan's fighting services were undergoing rapid expansion. On 10th February war was formally declared. The first shots had been exchanged nearly forty-eight hours earlier, however, and what happened held ominous portents of Pearl Harbor thirty-eight years later.

Greatly inferior to her huge Russian adversary in manpower and material, Japan's one hope lay in obtaining command of the sea and control of Korea at the outset. By these two means the Russians would be deprived of any South Korean port from which to operate against Japan; harbours on the west coat of Korea would be available as bases for the Japanese fleet, and Japanese troops could be sent to Manchuria – both by sea and overland through Korea – before the Russians had time to bring overwhelming forces from Europe to fight them. To gain these advantages Japan struck before declaring war. A Russian ship in the neutral Korean port of Chemulpo was sunk and

Japanese troops landed in Korea. Meanwhile, the main Japanese fleet under Admiral Togo was steaming towards Port Arthur and shortly before midnight on 8th February, three Russian battleships were torpedoed by Japanese destroyers which attacked them while at anchor. At noon the following day a second attack was launched and four Russian cruisers were hit. Togo then blockaded the port and when, after a five months' siege, it was captured by Japanese troops the remnants of the Russian fleet fell into his hands.

Several months before Port Arthur fell the Russians had sent their main fleet from the Baltic to raise the blockade. It took seven months for this armada to reach the battle zone and it was wiped out in one day in the Straits of Tsushima. Considered by some naval historians to be the greatest sea engagement since Trafalgar, this historic battle won for Admiral Togo the title of Nelson of Japan. In the eyes of the world it also raised Japan's prestige to such an extent that she was promptly recognised as having achieved the status of one of the great powers. The fruits of victory included Korea, which became a Japanese protectorate, and virtual control of the southern half of Manchuria. But more important was something less tangible. By defeating the Russian colossus Japan had destroyed the myth of the White Man's invincibility and the Japanese were quick to turn the situation to their advantage.

In the years immediately following the war with Russia, Japan proceeded to consolidate her position on the mainland of East Asia and tighten her grip on southern Manchuria. As she did so her actions were being watched from Washington with growing apprehension. At the time of the war with Russia, Japan had received both moral and financial support from the United States, but before that her activities in the Pacific had been eyed with some suspicion. Resentment at the influx of Japanese labourers into the United States created further friction, and in the spring of 1905 a growing demand for the halting of Japanese immigration was coupled with agitation for the boycotting of Japanese firms in

Admiral Isoruku Yamamoto, C-in-C of the Combined Fleet of the Japanese
Imperial Navy until his death on 18th April 1943

America. President Roosevelt, who
had been urging the need of a strong
fleet as the best means of holding
Japan in check, regarded this anti-
Japanese agitation as provocative
and the height of folly on the part of
those who, only recently, had refused
to support his plea for a stronger
navy. However, by the conclusion of
an agreement in 1908, under which
the Japanese government consented
to co-operate in restricting the emi-
gration of Japanese labour to America,
the tension was eased and another
five years were to pass before the
immigration question reared its head
again.

The next two decades saw a spectacular increase in Japan's industrial,
commercial and economic strength.
During this time there was also a
gradual rise in the state of tension
between Japan and the United States
brought about by a competitive

struggle for naval supremacy in the
western Pacific. The naval armaments
race did not begin in real earnest until
1916 but it had been foreshadowed by
the turn of the century. With the
acquisition of Hawaii and the Philippines by the United States in 1898,
the need for a powerful fleet to protect them had become clear to all
thoughtful Americans. And in his
seven years in office President Roosevelt contrived to double the size of
the United States Navy – although he
failed to obtain more than a fraction
of the ships he asked for. Japan, for
her part, having built up a navy
strong enough to gain command of the
seas over her Russian adversary, continued to increase its strength after
victory had been won. By 1912 naval
expenditure accounted for thirty-
five per cent of the national budget,
and it would have been heavier if a
proposal for creating a new fleet of

eight great battleships and eight formidable cruisers had not been rejected. It was 1920 before this 8 – 8 programme, as it was called, was sanctioned, but expansion of the Imperial Navy had already started.

Although she was linked by treaty obligations to Britain, Japan could have remained neutral when the First World War broke out in Europe. She was not obliged to join in unless Germany attacked British possessions in the Far East. And this Germany had not done. But Japan decided to align herself with Britain and her assistance proved invaluable. Consequently at the end of the war she was rewarded by being given all the German islands in the Pacific north of the equator which she had occupied – the Caroline, Pelew, Marshall and Mariana groups. Thus provided with a strategically valuable position in mid-Pacific, Japan was now in a position to challenge the United States for control of that ocean. And just as the warship building race between Britain and Germany had been a factor contributing to the First World War, so the naval rivalry between Japan, the United States and Britain which followed, threatened to touch off another war. Throughout the 1920s Japan's naval power was governed by a 5-5-3 agreement which meant that for every five capital ships Britain and America built, Japan could build only three. The agreement, concluded in Washington in 1922, virtually relegated Japan to third power status and acceptance of the role of the Imperial Navy as that of a deterrent force. Initially the Japanese delegate to the conference, Admiral Kato, had demanded that the fleet ratio should be 10-10-7. But contemporary naval experts believed that a defending fleet must be fifty per cent stronger than its attackers and conceding the 10-7 ratio would mean losing a margin of superiority which could make all the difference between victory and defeat if Japan attacked America. Consequently, in terms of battleships the 5-5-3 ratio which Britain and America persuaded Japan to accept ensured continued United States superiority. Aircraft carriers, which were to decide the mastery of the Pacific, were not even considered at the conference because so few existed.

For some years Japan observed the letter of the Washington agreement – although the navy was expanded as near to the limitations of the agreement as was possible. But by 1930 militaristic factions in Japan were dreaming of an 'Asia for the Asiatics' under Japanese rule. And, as the 5-5-3 agreement stood in the way of expansion of Japan's naval power, there was a call for its renunciation or a more favourable ratio. Neither renunciation nor change in the ratio emerged from the London Disarmament Conference in 1930 and as the militants began to gain control of the Japanese government their criticism of this and the former agreement increased. A second Disarmament Conference had been scheduled to take place in London during 1935. But the outcry was such that it was decided to hold a preliminary conference in 1934. This conference, which turned out to be the last attempt to limit naval forces by treaty, was doomed to failure before it even started. Talks dragged on for two months but the Japanese delegation seemed determined not to reach any agreement. National self-determination of armaments as a sovereign right was what Japan demanded, and suggestions that the ratio might be continued while some compromise was worked out were firmly rejected. That autumn Japan declared that any extension of the Washington Treaty would be useless and gave notice that she was withdrawing from it. In Japan the new tough-policy group of military politicians had triumphed; it would be very difficult now to stop the onrushing waves of war.

Once the restrictions on its size and composition were removed Japan was free to expand her Imperial Navy as far as her financial resources permitted, and by the autumn of 1941 it was more powerful than the combined British and United States fleets in the Pacific area. Not only did Japan possess the two largest battleships the world had ever seen, she also had ten aircraft carriers while the United States had only three and the British one. Even more important the Imperial Navy had embraced the strategy of using the aircraft carrier as an offensive weapon whilst the United States was still thinking in terms of carriers as useful only to provide an air umbrella for battleships.

In 1931 Japan occupied northern Manchuria. According to the Japanese the decision to do so was forced upon them by the Chinese who had been arrogant and provocative. But the rapid extension of military operations soon showed that they had been planning to overrun the province for some time. The real reason was that the militants, who were now gaining control of Japan's government and whipping up patriotic fervour, had decided that Japan must expand. Her islands were a land of exceptional beauty, but their mountainous terrain lacked the raw materials to feed the modern industries on which the teeming millions of her exploding population depended. More and more territory was needed and six years after the occupation of Manchuria the Japanese began an invasion of China. For eight years, until 1945, this fighting continued.

By 1939 Japan was dedicated to war, and with every success of her armies in the great land mass of Asia, the grip of the militant clique tightened on her government. But as the generals dragged Japan deeper into northern China the admirals saw that she was being drawn nearer to a collision with Soviet Russia. In their view, if Japan was going to risk war with a major power then it must be in a direction in which she stood the best chance of success – and one in which the strength of the Imperial Navy could be exploited. Since Japan had been committed to a campaign on the Chinese mainland it seemed that the logical way to bring it to a successful conclusion was to employ the navy along China's seaboard, rather than letting the army advance north and risk the possibility of a head-on clash with the Soviet Union. In a succession of combined operations, the admirals contended, a relatively small army could be used effectively and flexibly against the numerically superior Chinese. Such tactics should pay double dividends. First, there was less chance of Japan getting bogged down in a war of attrition with two great land powers,

each of which had a population greater than her own. Second, the presence of a powerful Japanese navy operating in south-east Asia would bolster diplomatic and commercial attempts to expand in that region. For some time the Japanese had been trying to increase their trade with the oil-rich Dutch East Indies and as the strain of the war in China dragged on and sharpened the need for oil and other vital raw materials the admirals themselves had come to regard this area as vital to them.

Up to 1938 the Japanese had always regarded Soviet Russia as Japan's principal potential enemy. But growing resentment with the diplomatic pressure applied by the United States to stop the war with China led to Russia being displaced by America. The Imperial Navy, expanding rapidly, had never had any doubts as to who the real enemy would be in a major war. Japanese generals could see that if they continued to advance north into China, a clash with Russia must come sooner or later. Japanese admirals, on the other hand, knew that an advance south would bring friction with the United States and that war with America would be a sea war. They did not relish the prospect any more than their counterparts in the United States. But the generals were in control and they branded negotiations with the United States as 'soft diplomacy'.

Bloated from their Chinese conquests and feeling all-powerful, the army leaders were for war and the promotion of a 'Greater East Asia Co-prosperity Sphere'. Hitler and Mussolini were urging Japan to join them in a defensive three-power pact and the generals were in favour of doing so. Most of the admirals were not. But the situation changed when President Roosevelt ordered the US Pacific Fleet to leave its West Coast ports and concentrate at Pearl Harbor. He had already imposed economic sanctions against Japan and these were beginning to bite, but the move of the US fleet suggested that the President was considering an armed intervention. When, in July 1941, US trade with Japan was severed and Japanese assets in the US frozen, war seemed imminent.

Admiral Yamamoto

Isoruku Yamamoto was appointed Commander-in-Chief of the Japanese Combined fleet – the *rengo Kantai* – on 30th August 1939. The appointment was the senior executive command in the Imperial Navy, and it is said that Yamamoto, a teetotaler, was so surprised when he heard that he had been selected to fill it that he drank a whole glass of beer in one gulp. Two weeks after his appointment the Germans invaded Poland and the Second World War began. Yamamoto knew that Japan was bound to become involved sooner or later, and he threw himself into the job of preparing the Imperial Navy for war with his customary ruthless drive. 'Under my command,' he announced, 'priority will be given to air training.' Already his mind was beginning to revolve round the problem of how to destroy the American Pacific Fleet if Japan's politicians should be so unwise as to involve her in a war with the United States.

Because Yamamoto was flatly opposed to such a war, the circumstances under which he conceived and pushed through the plan to strike at Pearl Harbor are ironical. His outspokenness against policies which brought the risk of such a war had already caused Japanese political extremists to accuse him of being pro-American and a traitor. In his previous position as Vice-Minister to the Imperial Navy he had been threatened with assassination because of his anti-war beliefs. But Yamamoto had seen America's industrial might at first hand when he studied at Harvard University, and later when he served as naval attaché in Washington. He believed, as did most people of Japan at the time, that the Japanese were a chosen race, destined to play the dominant role in Asia. Realism contained his patriotism however, and he feared the consequences of a war with America and Britain. As the Navy's Vice-Minister his often expressed view was that such a war could end only in disaster. How was it possible then that such a man could engineer the devastating stroke that precipitated such a war? The answer is that Isoruku Yamamoto had no alternative; he was a prisoner of history. Born of impoverished

Samurai stock, his very nature demanded that he should follow the traditions of *Bushido*. Duty to his Emperor and to Japan had priority over everything else. As Commander-in-Chief, Yamamoto's responsibility was the protection of his homeland. If others decided on war, he had to be ready for it.

As far back as 1927 Yamamoto had recognised air power as a crucial new element of naval strategy and when he was appointed to the new aircraft carrier *Akagi* the following year he devoted himself – as one of his biographers has phrased it – 'to the practical problems involved in the developing theories of air warfare'. A captain at the age of thirty-nine, a rear-admiral at forty-four, Navy Vice-Minister in 1937, it was not until he became Commander-in-Chief that he was able to exert much influence on the strategic thinking of the Imperial Navy. After the London Disarmament Conference of 1934 – at which Yamamoto had been the principal Japanese delegate – Japan had embarked on an extensive programme of battleship construction designed to give Japan superiority in capital ships. Four giant battleships, each equipped with nine 18.1-inch guns were planned. (The first of these monsters, the *Yamato*, was completed in December 1941 and the second, the *Musashi*, eight months later. The third vessel, the *Shinano*, became the world's biggest aircraft carrier; construction of the fourth was abandoned.) As the United States was unlikely to build ships which could not pass through the Panama Canal a tonnage lead should ensure Japan's victory in any naval engagement which followed the classical concept. In peace, the new giants would enhance Japan's international standing and provide great bargaining power in negotiations with the United States and Britain; in an emergency they would serve as 'iron security'.

Among the admirals only Yamamoto lacked enthusiasm about the building of these great ships. In his view they were obsolete even before their keels were laid. 'They are like elaborate religious scrolls which old people hang up in their homes. They are of no proven worth. They are

purely a matter of faith – not reality,' he said. '. . . They will be as much use to Japan in modern warfare as a *Samurai* sword . . .' In his view it would be aircraft carriers, surrounded and protected by cruisers and destroyers, which would provide the key to sea supremacy in naval battles of the future. The money spent on the monster battleships would be better spent on carriers and aircraft.

Challenged by his colleagues, Yamamoto insisted that attacks by torpedo-carrying aircraft would probably prove the most effective method of destroying battleships. 'The finest serpent,' he said, quoting an old Japanese proverb: 'may be overcome by a swarm of ants.' Pearl Harbor was to justify his prophetic words.

Despite the entrenched opposition Yamamoto's imaginative ideas gradually began to be accepted. At his insistence two new carriers (the 30,000-ton, 34-knot *Shokaku* and *Zuikaku*) were built; long-range flying boats capable of carrying a 2,000 pound bomb load 800 miles (and whose performance in 1938 on a bombing raid from Kigushu to Shanghai astonished Western navies) came into service. In great secrecy also a new and revolutionary fighter aircraft was put into production. (For two years this plane, the Mitsubishi A6M Zero, was to dominate the Pacific.) None of these developments were accomplished without difficulties, and American magazines assured their readers that Japanese ships and aircraft were no match for those of the United States. Japanese pilots suffered from the world's highest casualty rate, ran one report in *Aviation*. Furthermore the same report concluded: 'America's aviation experts can say without hesitation that the chief military airplanes of Japan are either outdated already or are becoming outdated . . .' Another magazine told its readers: 'The Japanese navy air force consists of four carriers with 200 airplanes.' Like Britain's assessment of the strength of Germany's cardboard tanks in the days before Dunkirk, the international

Admiral Togo, Japan's Nelson, whose operation at Port Arthur in 1898 set the pattern for Pearl Harbor

evaluation of Japanese airpower was sadly mistaken.

Within two months of becoming Commander-in-Chief, Yamamoto had initiated the first of a series of changes in the basic strategic plan of the Imperial Navy. In 1909, when a 'National Defence Policy' had been formulated in which the United States became hypothetical Enemy No 1, a decisive engagement in the Western Pacific had been envisaged. Believing that the Americans would take the offensive in the Western Pacific, the Japanese planned to destroy the US fleet in home waters. On an Inner South Seas line, somewhere between island groups of the Marianas and the Marshalls, the Imperial Navy would fight this battle, and for over thirty years the Imperial Navy had trained for it. Japanese warships were specifically designed to operate in the rough seas around Japan and the idea of sending them to distant Hawaii had never been considered seriously. Yamamoto's first change in the plan was to extend the proposed battle area eastwards to include the Marshalls. As the change seemed to be a minor one and of no apparent significance it was accepted without question by the Naval General Staff.

Yamamoto's next move was to make the Combined Fleet true to its name. When he took over, its two components were operating separately. Under his direct operational command he brought them together, combining aircraft carriers, battleships, cruisers and ancillary vessels in a single mighty fleet. In the spring of 1940 the first manoeuvres to take place under his command were staged, and in these the new Commander-in-Chief stressed the need to improve the training in attacks by carrier-based aircraft on ships. Judging by what he had seen he said that considerably more training was necessary. This was nearly two years before Pearl Harbor and the tough training programme was the direct result of Yamamoto's address. By December 1941 Japanese naval pilots had reached a very high standard of proficiency.

Citing the growing influence of air power as evinced by the recent manoeuvres, Yamamoto now pushed the boundary of the strategic plan's battle area still further east – this time, significantly, all the way to Hawaii. Again the Naval General Staff raised no objections. Hawaii had always been included in the master plan as the area of operations for an advance expeditionary force of submarines. By this time, Yamamoto was convinced that the politicians were dragging Japan towards a war with the United States. Sooner or later the Japanese army would move south to break the deadlock in China by escalating the inconclusive fighting there into a war throughout Greater East Asia. Japan was desperately short of oil and if the oil resources of the Dutch East Indies were cut off even his aircraft would be immobilised. Yet, as Yamamoto read the situation, a move south against the British and Dutch colonies would mean war with the United States, and although the American Pacific Fleet could be discounted as a threat to Japan proper, it would be a potential menace to Japan's expeditionary forces in the south. The only way to secure their lines of communication would be to destroy the US fleet at its base. To Admiral Ryunsuke Kusaka, Yamamoto confided: 'If we are ordered to fight the United States we might be able to score a runaway victory and hold our own for six months or a year. But in the second year the Americans will increase their strength and it will be very difficult for us to fight on with any prospects of final victory.' He did not reveal to Kusaka what he had in mind. But it was implicit in what he said.

Yamamoto's idea of a surprise attack on Pearl Harbor undoubtedly stemmed from Admiral Togo's action at Port Arthur. But such a possibility had first been considered by an *American* admiral. In 1932, the retiring commander of the United States Pacific Fleet, Admiral Frank A Schofield, had suggested that an imaginary enemy in the Pacific might decide to concentrate a carrier force

Above right: Akagi, the aircraft carrier which was Yamamoto's first command in 1927. *Centre right:* The giant battleship *Yamoto. Below right:* The carrier *Shokaku*

Mitsubishi A6M2 Zero-sen (Allied code name 'Zeke')
Engine: Nakajima *Sakae* 12, 940 hp at take off *Armament:* Two 7.7mm machine guns and two 20mm Type 99 Model 1 Mark 3 cannon and two 132 lbs bombs
Speed: 331·5 mph at 14,930 feet *Climb rate:* 19,685 feet in 7 minutes 27 seconds
Ceiling: 32,810 feet *Range:* 1,160 miles *Weight empty:* 3,704 lbs *Weight loaded:* 5,313 lbs *Span:* 39 feet 4½ inches *Length:* 29 feet 8¾ inches

and raid Hawaii or the West Coast of the United States before declaring war. Up to that time the force of thirty-eight aircraft based on Pearl Harbor had been judged to be adequate for the defence of the base. To prove this, the newly built carriers *Saratoga* and *Lexington* sailed across the Pacific, and sixty miles north-east of Oahu, 150 aircraft were launched into the pre-dawn dark of a

misty morning. In heavy seas th[e] ships were pitching and rolling – jus[t] as the Japanese carriers were to d[o] nine years later. Emerging from th[e] clouds above their target, undetecte[d] and unchallenged, the aircraft dive[d] in mock attacks on the collection o[f] ships in Pearl Harbor and the attack[-] ers were judged to have been wholl[y] successful. For a few days this out[-] come caused some consternation i[n]

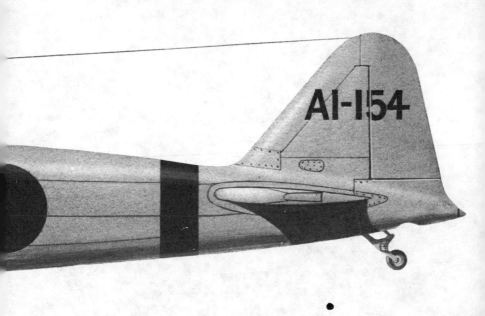

United States naval circles. Then, with Schofield's retirement and Press concern with other matters in those piping days of peace, the flurry subsided and the problem was conveniently forgotten. But not by the air-conscious Yamamoto.

During 1940 the feasibility of using torpedo-carrying aircraft to attack ships in port was ably demonstrated in the Mediterranean. To the Italians, who tried to sink the cruiser HMS *Gloucester* in Alexandria harbour must go the credit for being the first to attempt this novel form of attack. Unsuccessful though it was, they had shown its possibilities and the British were quick to follow up the lesson.

On 11th November, the Italian fleet riding at anchor in the Italian base at Taranto was crippled in a daring attack by two waves of slow-flying old Swordfish biplanes from the carrier HMS *Illustrious*. For a British loss of only two aircraft the Italian navy received a blow from which it never fully recovered, and in little more than an hour the entire balance of naval power in the Mediterranean was altered in favour of Britain. To Yamamoto it seemed that his theories had been tested and proved. 'Operation Z' was now conceived.

Above: USS Saratoga. Below: USS Lexington

'Operation Z': the Pearl Harbor plan

The Hawaiian islands in the North Pacific ocean lie 2,090 nautical miles south-west of San Francisco. As the name implies, the principal island is Hawaii. But the capital of Honolulu is located on the smaller island of Oahu which is characterised by mountain ranges at its eastern and western edges. Honolulu and the American naval base of Pearl Harbor lie between these mountains. The population is a mixture of Caucasians, Japanese, Chinese and Filipinos among whom there has been a considerable amount of inter-marriage; in 1941 about ninety per cent of this population were citizens of the United States.

For many years the Americans had appreciated that Pearl Harbor had all the natural attributes of a conveniently located harbour, well suited to the strategic deployment of the United States Navy. And in August 1919 it was inaugurated as a base, although a United States fleet was not stationed there permanently until as late as 1940. 'Pearl' was never popular with the sailors for, as Rear-Admiral Samuel E Morrison pointed out: 'White women were few in numbers, and the shopkeepers gypped the men . . .' Nor for that matter was the base popular with the admirals. Apart from logistic problems arising from the fact that it had to be supplied directly from the west coast of America 3,000 miles away, the security of a land-locked harbour with only one entrance was a constant nagging worry. By sinking only one ship in the single entrance channel the harbour could be bottled up. Three hours were needed to get the fleet out of harbour through the entry channel to the open sea and with the fleet in port the congestion of ships, fuel, repair installations and supply dumps made the harbour a seductive target for an attack from the air. Yet in May 1940, when Washington decided that a battle fleet should be kept in Hawaiian waters to deter the Japanese, there was no alternative anywhere in the area which offered the same facilities as Pearl Harbor. Admiral Joseph O Richardson, Commander-in-Chief in May 1940, questioned the wisdom of the decision to base the fleet on Pearl more or less 'permanently'. Richardson argued that it would be safer to return to better bases on the west coast of America. When he pressed his objection as far as the President, Richardson was relieved of his command and replaced by Admiral Husband E Kimmel.

Nobody in the Imperial Navy knew the problems of Pearl Harbor better than Admiral Yamamoto. Hanging on the bulkhead in the cabin of his flagship *Nagato* was an up-to-date map of the base, which carried the marks of his special interest, and in a locked drawer of his desk was an impressively bound summary of the mass of information about the base which Japanese Intelligence had accumulated. Under the grandiose title *The Habits, Strengths and Defences of the American Fleet in the Hawaiian Area*, this volume contained topographical descriptions, charts of the Hawaiian waters, details of the military, naval and defence installations, schedules from which a pattern of the American air and sea patrols could be established, the rhythm of ship movements, and the customary procedures regarding crew relief and 'liberty' while ships were in harbour. From its pages Yamamoto could derive a complete picture of the day-to-day life of the base. As he also knew that the American fleet now stationed at Pearl Harbor was there for training purposes only, Yamamoto appreciated that this picture of life in the American base was not likely to vary very much. A training programme did not admit much flexibility. Of necessity ships operated on a regular routine – going to sea for fixed periods to exercise and remaining in port between times. Provided the training programme was adhered to and no strategic deployment was ordered it ought to be possible to predict when the largest concentration of warships would be in the harbour. Furthermore the configuration of the base which imposed such a strict limitation on vessels entering or leaving the harbour was as much a boon to a prospective attacker as it was a headache to the commander-in-chief of the United States fleet. Unless the Americans effected some radical improvements in the air defences of

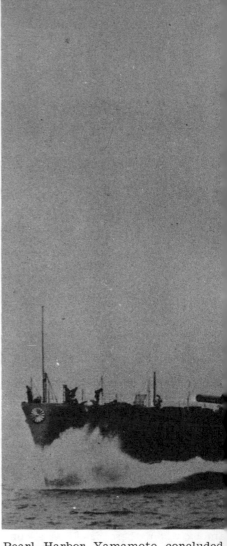

Pearl Harbor Yamamoto concluded that the chances of success of an air strike were excellent. As we have seen, for the loss of only two of their number, twenty-four British aircraft had sunk three Italian battleships at Taranto; given an element of surprise, a raid on a bigger scale promised even greater prizes at Pearl Harbor.

Even the surprise element should not be too difficult to attain. For the greater part of the year the prevailing winds in the Hawaiian area are the north-east trades. These are deflected upwards by the peaks of the Koolau Range overlooking Pearl Harbor on

Nagato, **Yamamoto's flagship**

easterly side, to form banks of cumulus around the pinnacles and bringing rain to the windward slopes. But in the so-called rainy months the wind occasionally shifts to the north and blows down the valley. When this happens there are scattered clouds and sometimes rain over Honolulu and Pearl Harbor, as well as the banks of cumulus over the mountains. Such conditions could provide cover for a raiding force breaking in from the north and serve to confuse the anti-aircraft defences of the base.

On the other side of the world the importance of the British attack on Taranto was not lost on the United States Navy. In a memorandum to Army Secretary Henry L Stimson, Navy Secretary Frank Knox said: 'The success of the British aerial torpedo attack against ships at anchor suggests that precautionary measures be taken immediately to protect Pearl Harbor against a surprise attack in the event of war between the United States and Japan. The greatest danger will come from the aerial torpedo. The highest priority must

23

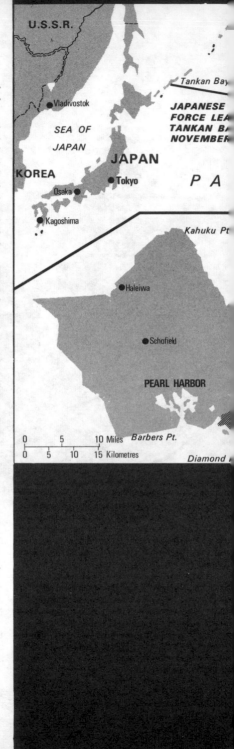

The route of the Japanese task force from the rendezvous at Tankan Bay in the Kuriles to the start point for the attack on Pearl Harbor

be given to getting more interceptor aircraft, AA guns and additional radar equipment.'

Stimson agreed and the Hawaiian command was ordered to strengthen its defences against a possible surprise air attack. A month later, in December 1940, Admiral Kimmel, the commander-in-chief of the fleet based at Pearl Harbor, told Washington that 'Anti-torpedo nets at Pearl Harbor would restrict boat traffic by narrowing the channel.' By this decision Kimmel had doomed most of his big battleships.

At about the same time as Kimmel rejected the precaution of torpedo nets, Yamamoto first confided his ideas for an attack on Pearl Harbor to his chief-of-staff, Admiral Shigeru Fukudome. Until then he had chosen not to confide in his staff, although the fact that he had initiated a vigorous training programme for the pilots of his carriers is evidence that his ideas had crystallised. Yamamoto had kept his secret to himself. The aim of his air training programme which simulated attacks in a confined valley was justified to the pilots and carrier captains as practice for support of army operations on land. Similar support had been given in 1937 at Nanking by the navy's carrier-borne aircraft, and Yamamoto said that the present pilots lacked experience and training in attacks on land targets. Like a film director seeking the location of a suitable set, Yamamoto himself had sailed along Japanese coast until he discovered a place suited to his needs. South of Kyushu in Kagoshima Bay the terrain bore a strong resemblance to Pearl Harbor and the fleet carriers were moved to Kyushu. But day after day as the aircraft skimmed over the bay to practice releasing their torpedoes and bombs at a low altitude no-one yet knew the real purpose of their training.

In his own mind Yamamoto had settled one thing, the code name for the projected operation. 'Operation Z' it would be, after Admiral Togo's

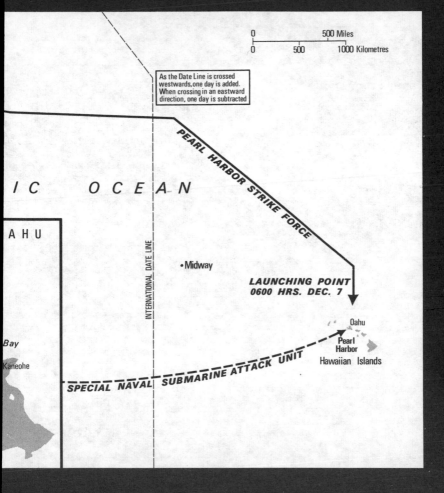

0   500 Miles
0   500   1000 Kilometres

As the Date Line is crossed westwards, one day is added. When crossing in an eastward direction, one day is subtracted

PEARL HARBOR STRIKE FORCE

I C   O C E A N

A H U

INTERNATIONAL DATE LINE

• Midway

LAUNCHING POINT
0600 HRS. DEC. 7

Oahu
Pearl Harbor
Hawaiian Islands

Bay
Kaneohe

SPECIAL NAVAL SUBMARINE ATTACK UNIT

Rear-Admiral Takijuro Onishi, Chief of Staff of the 11th Air Fleet

famous 'Z' signal made on the eve of the battle of Tsushima Strait thirty-six years before. 'The rise or fall of the nation is at stake in this battle.' It was Yamamoto's way of venerating the memory of the hero of his youth. To turn his ideas into reality he now began to solicit the opinion of selected colleagues. The first to whom he turned was Rear-Admiral Takijuro Onishi, one of the Imperial Navy's few air-minded officers, who at the end of the war was to become the organiser of the first *Kamikaze* units. As chief of staff of the 11th Air Fleet of land-based bombers Onishi had already contemplated the idea of an attack on Hawaii from Japanese bases in the Marshalls – an impossible feat because of the distances involved. Yamamoto was confident that Onishi's approach to his idea would not be hampered by conventional operational thinking and that if he thought the plan was feasible he would say so. The fundamentals of his plan were outlined to Onishi. Yamamoto wanted to cripple the US Pacific Fleet with one surprise blow as a preliminary to operations designed to capture the oil areas of south-east Asia. Outwardly impassive, Onishi listened and then asked permission to consult Commander Minoru Genda, a brilliant and experienced air staff officer serving on the carrier *Kaga* at Kyushu. Thirty-six years old, Genda had just completed a tour of duty as assistant naval attaché in London and in this capacity had reported on the Taranto operation. In common with Onishi and Yamamoto, Genda showed a belief in the supremacy of naval air power, and because of his familiarity with the attack on Taranto it was to be expected that he would favour the projected 'Operation Z'. For ten days he studied it thoughtfully and then reported back to Onishi with his conclusions: 'The plan is difficult but not impossible.'

Initially Yamamoto had intended to concentrate his attack on American battleships. He knew that carriers were superior as striking units but as most Americans – like most Japanese – still considered that battleships were the backbone of the fleet he felt that their destruction would deal a more paralysing blow to the Americans. Initially also, he had toyed with the idea of the attacking aircraft being unable to return to their carriers. By launching the planes outside their operational range the 'flat-tops' would not need to approach so close to Hawaii, and could turn for home the instant the planes had taken off. After the strike the pilots could crash-land in the water and be rescued by destroyers and submarines. Neither of these ideas found favour with Genda. The prime target, he said, would have to be the American carriers since they were the greatest potential menace to the Imperial Navy. And, for the best results, the Japanese carriers would have to approach as close as possible to Pearl Harbor. A suicidal form of attack would have a bad psychological effect on the pilots, and at a critical stage in the war Japan could afford to lose neither aircraft nor pilots. Moreover, steaming back without aircraft would hazard the carriers if the Americans counterattacked.

One factor favouring the operation was the Imperial Navy's adequacy of aircraft carriers. The 36,500 ton *Akagi* was one of the most formidable carriers in the world, larger even than America's *Lexington* and *Saratoga* and after her refit of 1936–1938 she could carry ninety-one aircraft. Similar to the *Akagi* was the 38,200 ton *Kaga*. Two smaller carriers, the *Hiryu* and *Soryu*, displacing 17,300 tons and 15,900 tons respectively, were also in service. Two other carriers, each of 25,675 tons, the *Zuikaku* and *Shokaku*, were expected to be commissioned in August 1941 and this would raise the total of fleet carriers to six. Genda's view was that all six must be used in 'Operation Z'. To Onishi he also made two other points: only the most competent officers and best trained pilots should be selected for the task, and that the operation should be kept a close secret until the very last moment before the attack.

With Yamamoto's approval, Onishi now set Genda to work on a draft plan for the operation and towards the end of March it was beginning to

take shape. The attack would be mounted by a special task force, comprising an advance expeditionary force of about twenty I-class and five midget submarines with their supporting screen, together with a main strike force built around the six carriers. This strike force would take a circuitous route, avoiding known shipping routes which would bring them to within 230 miles of Hawaii. From here the aircraft would take off from their carriers and fly towards Pearl Harbor along an air corridor in which it was believed that American air patrols were few and far between. An estimated force of 360 aircraft would be needed which should include dive-bombers, high-level bombers, torpedo-bombers and fighters. Because they were more destructive than bombs and more accurate on a short run-in, torpedoes would probably be the most efficient weapon to use against the American ships. Unfortunately this raised a technical problem. Pearl Harbor was so shallow that the conventional Japanese torpedoes in current service would strike the bottom if launched in the normal way. Since the depth of water in Taranto harbour was forty-two feet or less, and the British had been able to sink ships with their air launched torpedoes it was clear that the problem could be resolved, for Pearl Harbor was forty-five feet deep. Bombs of over three times the usual weight would also be needed to pierce the deck armour of the American battleships. Finally, surprise was essential if the operation was to succeed. Without the surprise element there was the risk of severe losses to the task force during its long and vulnerable return voyage to Japan. To be sure of the element of surprise the United States should have no warning of the imminence of hostilities.

Onishi himself estimated that 'Operation Z' had about a sixty per cent chance of success; other senior officers co-operating during the planning stages were not so optimistic. Some, including Admiral Fukudome, con-

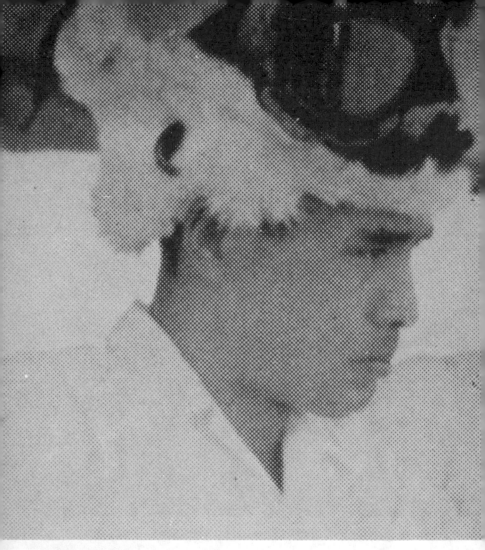

Above left: Commander Minoru Genda, the man who was primarily responsible for the execution of the Pearl Harbor plan 'Operation Z'. Genda survived the war to become the Chief of Staff of the post-war Japanese air force, a member of the Japanese parliament, and a firm friend of the United States.
Right: Rear-Admiral Chuichi Nagumo, commander of the Pearl Harbor task force

sidered it downright reckless and when opposition to the operation was raised by the Naval General Staff their opinions were based mainly on Fukudome's views. Later he admitted that if he, and not Onishi, had been entrusted with the planning of 'Operation Z', he would have recommended that Yamamoto should abandon the idea. Despite Fukudome's lack of enthusiasm and Onishi's doubts, Yamamoto was convinced that a carrier-borne air assault on Pearl Harbor was feasible. By the end of March the planning was in an advanced stage and the question of who should command the task force set up for the assault was now raised. Yamamoto would clearly have loved to have commanded it himself. But

this was not possible; as commander-in-chief of the combined fleet he had too many other responsibilities and someone junior to himself had to be appointed. The choice fell on Rear-Admiral Chuichi Nagumo, a hard-bitten unimaginative old sailor who knew nothing about aircraft or air-craft carriers, but he was the senior rear-admiral and next in line for promotion. His only claim to any specialist knowledge was on the sub-ject of navigation, and on learning that he was expected to take a huge fleet across thousands of miles of the Pacific Ocean almost to the gates of

an enemy fortress, refuelling en route, without being detected and on a tight schedule, he was appalled. As the success of the operation largely depended on the element of surprise he could see that if anything went wrong Japan stood to lose a large proportion of the Imperial Navy – for which he would be blamed. For the time being, the owlish Nagumo took comfort in the thought that the operation was unlikely ever to mate-rialise. As yet, war with the United States was by no means certain, and the plan had not yet had the approval of the Japanese High Command.

War becomes inevitable

Despite Nagumo's hopes, Japan continued her inexorable march towards war with the United States. Taking advantage of France's defeat by the Germans, the Japanese made their first move beyond China in 1940. Claiming that important supplies were reaching Chiang Kai-shek's forces by way of French Indo-China, they insisted that the Indo-Chinese northern border must be controlled by Japanese troops. German pressure on the government of Vichy France, combined with Japanese threats addressed to the colony's governor, resulted in the latter agreeing to the occupation of northern Indo-China. Then, when troops were installed there, further pressure led to the governor's acceptance of a 'protectorate' over the whole of Indo-China and the Japanese moved swiftly south to take over the rest of the country. From the air and naval bases which now became available to them in Indo-China, the Japanese troops were well placed for further advances into Siam, and the Siamese government was invited to emulate Indo-China's example and accept Tokyo's 'protection'.

'If need be,' declared the War Minister Hideki Tojo when the decision to occupy Indo-China was announced in the Japanese parliament, 'we accept war with Britain and the United States.' However, as it was patently obvious that neither Britain nor America was prepared to go to war to recover Indo-China for the Vichy French, these words were not such a provocative challenge as they might seem. Neither country wanted war. Nevertheless the move of powerful Japanese forces into a critical and strategic area of south-east Asia aroused considerable alarm as well as anger, and within forty-eight hours of the extension of the Japanese occupation, the United States, Britain and Holland froze Japanese assets and imposed trade embargoes on Japan. A few days later President Roosevelt barred all further shipments of oil to Japan, and Holland followed by prohibiting supplies from the oilfields of the Dutch East Indies.

President Roosevelt, whose decision to impose an oil embargo on Japan resulted in Japan's decision to seize the oil fields of the Dutch East Indies

'Economic war has been declared,' said a Japanese newspaper in an article stressing the country's vulnerability to the oil embargo. Confronted with an economic blockade Japan faced slow but sure strangulation, and unless the oil embargo were lifted the need to seize the oilfields of the Dutch East Indies was a matter of life and death for the Imperial Navy. With sufficient stocks of oil for only a few months, the question was not so much whether they must be seized, but how much time was left in which to do it. Confronted with this situation the naval chiefs bluntly told the Prime Minister that it must be resolved by October at the latest; war or peace, Japan must have oil.

Fuminaro Konoye, the prime minister, was a hereditary prince and a man with all the exquisite manners and

Left: Prince Fuminaro Konoye, the Japanese Prime Minister at the time of the US imposition of sanctions.
Below: US Secretary of State Cordell Hull (left) and the US Ambassador to Japan, Joseph C Grew (right)

fine personal qualities of a cultured Japanese nobleman. But he was not the man to lead his restive country at this juncture of history. It was Konoye's impetuosity that had manoeuvred the nation into a position from which there was virtually no alternative to war and having got it into this situation he was frightened by the shadows he had conjured up. In Washington, Japan's ambassador, the one-eyed Admiral Nomura, was grappling hopelessly with diplomatic problems far beyond his experience as a sailor and having little success with Cordell Hull, the American Secretary of State. (Athough important Dutch and British interests were at stake, these negotiations were an all-American affair.) In the past few months the attitude of the United States had hardened and she was now insisting not only on the evacuation of Japanese forces from Indo-China but also on them pulling out of China. But a general withdrawal of this magnitude could not be accomplished without destroying the morale of the Imperial Army, the generals had told Konoye;

he must reject the proposal firmly and squarely. Any concessions must come from America. But Cordell Hull was equally unyielding. He believed that the time had come to get tough; Japan could have peace with honour but it would have to be peace without empire. Hull remembered the humiliation and failure of Britain at Munich and was determined that the United States would not embark on a policy of appeasement with Japan. Influencing him, too, was a view prevalent in America, that Japan's strength had been drained in China. (This was wishful thinking, fed on exaggerated reports issued by the Chiang Kai-shek government of the scale of Chinese resistance and the extent of Japanese casualties. The truth was soon to be seen that Japan was in 1941 only just approaching her full military potential, and only a part of it had been committed to China.) Finally, when the American experts reported that economic sanctions would bring the Japanese to heel, Cordell Hull decided to stand firm; American forces in the Far East were being reinforced and he considered that time was on the side of the United States.

With diplomatic negotiations in Washington deadlocked and the navy chiefs' ultimatum hanging over him like a Damoclean sword, Konoye attempted to try a direct approach to the United States. Through the American ambassador in Tokyo, Joseph Grew, he suggested a summit conference in Hawaii between himself and President Roosevelt. When it was announced in the Japanese parliament, the proposal was decried on the grounds that such a meeting would upset Japan's Axis ally, Germany – although the military junta who objected to the visit did not actually veto it. Nor was it better received in America and any hopes Konoye may have held for a top level confrontation were extinguished when the United States government rejected his proposal. The American reply, on 3rd September, stipulated that before such a meeting could be considered there must be some preliminary and substantial measure of agreement between the two governments.

Pressed by the Japanese High Command for a decision before October and distressed by the American note, Konoye now sought the advice of his Emperor. The Prime Minister realised that he had little hope of persuading the military to give up their plans to extend the operations to the South Pacific, but he hoped that Hirohito might order them to do so. On 5th September, the day before an Imperial conference had been called, Konoye had a private audience with the Emperor. When Hirohito was told of the likely trend of events he was horrified. 'You mean to tell me,' he queried incredulously, 'that preparations for war are taking precedence over diplomatic negotiations?' Konoye admitted that this was so and said he hoped that His Majesty would intervene. Without further ado, General Sugiyama and Admiral Nagano, the army and navy chiefs-of-staff, were summoned to the royal presence to face a penetrating inquisition. How long would it take to conclude a successful campaign in the southern region, the Emperor asked. Three months was the estimate, Sugiyama replied. Icily, the Emperor retorted that he recalled that Sugiyama had assured him that a war with China would be short lived, yet after four years hand fighting was still going strong. 'The Chief of Staff,' Konoye wrote later, 'hung his head, unable to answer.' At this point Admiral Nagano came to the aid of his colleague. The situation was critical, he told the Emperor; both he and Sugiyama were in favour of negotiating with America, but something must be done quickly. If the negotiations failed it was their duty to see that Japan was prepared for the worst. 'You mean,' the Emperor asked – seeking an unambiguous assurance 'that the High Command is, now as before, giving precedence to diplomacy?' Both Sugiyama and Nagano assured His Majesty that this was so.

At the Imperial conference next day, Hirohito remained silent and seemingly impassive as Konoye read out his Cabinet's proposed plan of national policy. Traditionally the

General Tojo formally presents the text of an Imperial rescript to Emperor Hirohito

Emperor's 'divine radiance' barred him from taking an active part in the proceedings, and it was left to Baron Yoshimichi Hara, President of the Privy Council to speak for Hirohito. 'We have the impression,' he told the conference, 'that all hopes of peace have now been abandoned and that the emphasis is now on war rather than diplomacy in Japan's future course . . .' The Minister for the Imperial Navy, old Admiral Oikawa, hastily reassured Baron Hara that diplomacy still had priority over war. But Sugiyama and Nagano said nothing. There was a brief silence and then, to the astonishment of all present the Emperor himself rose to address the conference. 'We regret deeply,' he said, 'that the High Command has not seen fit to clarify the question before us.' Glancing at a small piece of paper he had taken from his pocket, he continued 'Our ancestor, Meiji Tenno, once wrote a poem part of which we are going to read to you now: '*Since we are all brothers in this world, why are the waves and winds so unsettled today?*' We have read this poem over and over again, and we are determined to make the Meiji idea of peace prevail in the world.' His audience was visibly shaken—not so much by the implication of the Emperor's words as by the fact that he considered the situation serious enough to warrant speaking at all—and silence ensued for some minutes after Hirohito had resumed his seat. Finally Admiral Nagano rose to assure the Emperor that the members of the High Command remained loyal to the throne, were disturbed by thoughts of incurring the Emperor's displeasure and recognised the importance of diplomacy. He and his fellow chiefs only contemplated the use of force of arms as a last resort, he said. After this the meeting adjourned as Konoye wrote, 'in an atmosphere of unprecedented tenseness'.

Despite his unprecedented intervention, there were those who preferred to believe that the Emperor had accepted the 'national plan' – albeit reluctantly. It had been announced and Hirohito had not formally vetoed it. Whether he could have done so is a matter of opinion. Already he had

gone just about as far as his subtle and complex authority would permit without prejudicing his position as the 'Son of Heaven'. Furthermore, at this juncture the Emperor knew nothing of the projected attack on Pearl Harbor, for despite their professed loyalty to the throne both Sugiyama and Nagano were deceiving him. By mid-August, army staffs were preparing the final detailed schedules for a war in the south, and naval forces – which had been already assigned to participate in these operations – were practicing the support of assult landing operations.

The annual naval war games, played with model ships at the Naval Staff College in Tokyo, were normally held in November or December. Because of the critical situation, however, a signal – sent under the joint authority of the naval chief of staff and the commander-in-chief of the combined fleet – had brought the 1941 games forward to mid-September. Three admirals, seven vice-admirals, six rear-admirals, seven captains and twenty commanders duly assembled in Tokyo and three days before Nagano's audience with the Emperor the games began. None of them knew that the games were to include Yamamoto's plan for a surprise attack on Pearl Harbor, until on 5th September he presented his Plan Z. Following the more conventional rehearsals of support operations mounted in co-operation with the army, he had expected that it would have a controversial reception, and his expectations were fully realised. Even in the preliminary discussion, no one was very enthusiastic about it. Almost everybody agreed it was a bold plan, some said it might even be feasible. But the main worry was how many carriers might be lost and a roll of a dice (which was the way the Japanese had of injecting into their games the inexplicable fortunes of war) showed two carriers sunk. Hardly anyone outside Yamamoto's own circle, and certainly no senior officer, came out in favour of the venture. Nevertheless it was agreed to run the plan as a game and the audience settled down to discuss the approach to Oahu. For this indefatigable Genda had worked out three possible routes: a southern route through the Marshalls, a central route passing south of Midway, and a northern course – of which the last was the one along which there was least likelihood of meeting other ships. As most of the Japanese ships had comparatively short cruising ranges they would have to be refuelled *en route* to Hawaii. Storms in the North Pacific, prevalent in the autumn and winter seasons would make this difficult, especially for smaller escort vessels like destroyers, which would have to refuel twice. For this reason Admiral Nagumo expressed his preference for the southern route. 'The weather will be against us,' he said. 'If you think so,' Genda pointed out, 'so too will the American admirals.' At this Nagumo agreed that the exercise should be based on a northern approach and in the event it was the northern passage between the Aleutians and Midway that was taken.

For the exercise proper the participants were divided into two teams, a blue team representing Japan, and a Red team the United States. In the first run-through the attack was judged to be a relative failure. Having acted according to the way the Japanese Intelligence had predicted the Americans would behave, the Red team had spotted Nagumo's forces during the morning of the attack and his aircraft had been intercepted by US fighters. The umpire decreed that half of Nagumo's aircraft had been shot down, whilst two carriers were sunk and other ships heavily damaged in an ensuing counter attack. Such an outcome was not likely to steel the apprehensive Nagumo's nerves. The second run-through was more successful. Approaching directly from the north on a careful schedule that gave the fleet the cover of darkness when they reached the operational limit of American reconnaissance aircraft, Nagumo's force was not spotted and the attack was a surprise. This time the umpires ruled that American losses were heavy, and the Japanese escaped almost unscathed.

This result did not mean that the opposition to Operation Z diminished. The admirals remained convinced the proposal was far too risky and likely to strain Japan's naval resources to the limit. The Naval General Staff had already completed a plan for the entire fleet to be employed in the southern invasion and as a body they were violently opposed to Yamamoto's venture. The Chief of Staff, Admiral Nagano, had wider doubts—'Why stir up America?' he argued. Like Yamamoto he had spent some time in the United States and had a healthy respect for both the Pacific Fleet and American industrial potential. 'Let us concentrate on taking Java and securing our supplies of oil,' he pleaded, 'then when the US Pacific Fleet sails into our home waters, *then* we will annihilate it.' Because Yamamoto fully shared Nagano's respect for the US navy, he was convinced that Japan's only chance was to smash it at once. If Japan was to wait for the Americans to collect their strength, there was every possibility that they would destroy the Japanese fleet first. Japan had enough carriers to strike at Pearl Harbor at the same time as she invaded Java, he contended. Why not stage both operations before the Pacific Fleet could attack? If the US Pacific Fleet were struck a mortal blow at Pearl Harbor, it could not be expected to reform before Japan had occupied the Philippines, Malaya and the East Indies.

The Naval General Staff persisted that the plan was too much of a gamble. Its sole chance of success depended on taking the American fleet by surprise, and if there was no surprise the attack would be a major disaster. But the underlying objection was the feeling that Operation Z ran contrary to the established and traditional character of naval warfare. The Japanese admirals, like American, British or German admirals for that matter, were steeped in the almighty power of the battleship. Their concept was one of duels with great capital ships, and for this very purpose Japan's fleet had been developed round the ten prewar battleships which placed her on a 3 to 5 firepower ratio with the United States. So strong had been the faith in the power of such leviathans and the invincibility of an armada built round them that two giant monsters, the *Yamato* and *Musashi*, were under construction and expected to be in service by early 1942. For more than twenty years the secret objective of the Japanese navy had been defined as the annihilation of the United States fleet, and time and time again the means and area for achieving this goal had been recognised as a surface battle between battleships in the vicinity of the Marshalls. Those whose confidence rested in the doctrine of the unsinkable strategic might of battleships distrusted the change to an air attack on Hawaii, and many of those who opposed Operation Z did so because they were honestly convinced that it was wrong to rely on a comparatively new arm which had only the successful British attack at Taranto to commend it.

The reluctant commander-designate, Nagumo, advanced another objection. He believed that Japan's aircraft carriers should be used to support the invasion of the vital oil regions. To his argument he added a prophetic warning that even the largest aircraft carrier could be effectively disabled by a few bombs. Nine months later at Midway his words were to be remembered. Yet not everyone was against the plan. Rear-Admiral Tamon Yamaguchi, one of the air arm admirals, supported it enthusiastically. If the US Pacific Fleet remained intact, he postulated, how could Japan ever exploit success in the south? Other younger officers, fired by the plan's sheer brash recklessness were overtly enthusiastic and wished to extend its scope. They wanted to follow up a strike with a landing to seize Pearl Harbor and occupy Oahu. This led to further arguments with the Naval General Staff who contended that all Japan's transports would be needed for the operations against the Dutch East Indies and Malaya. None could be spared for what would be a doubly risky operation. In this argument Yamamoto sided with the Naval General Staff. As it would be impossible to have the landing craft until the southern operations were completed, and this would probably take a month, it would be foolish to attempt a landing on Oahu. By that time the Americans would have had time to recover from the air attack on Pearl Harbor and the slow speed of an amphibious convoy would make the

initial landings extremely vulnerable to air and sea attack. Furthermore, even if the landings were successful the maintenance of a force at Oahu would present an insuperable supply problem.

Throughout September staff officers of the Naval General Staff and Yamamoto's Combined Fleet Headquarters met in a series of endless discussions on the overall operational commitments for the coming war. Operation Z was shelved as something about which no one could agree. Even Admiral Onishi had backed down after the war games, and he and the half-hearted Nagumo both earnestly counselled Yamamoto to give up the idea. Yamamoto, described in a biographical summary in American Intelligence files as 'exceptionally able, forceful . . . and a habitual winner at poker', rejected his colleagues' advice with passionate vehemence. However preposterous Operation Z might seem, Yamamoto's fanatical confidence in the validity of his arguments was such that if there had to be war with the United States he was prepared to stake his reputation and even his career on carrying it through. Whether he would have been so confident if he had been aware of the efficiency of American counter - intelligence is questionable.

During September the war games staff study containing the possibility of two carriers being sunk was published, and the controversy on the merits of an air attack on Pearl Harbor percolated down to officers serving with the Combined Fleet. On 11th October, to put an end to all rumours and bickering, Yamamoto summoned his senior officers to a conference on the flagship. After a congenial dinner, they were asked to voice, off the record, their objections to Operation Z. Encouraged by this unorthodox approach, the objectors spoke of their misgivings. A large proportion of the Imperial Navy would be committed to a perilous operation; if it failed the war would be lost before

Rear-Admiral Tamon Yamaguchi, one of the air-minded members of Yamamoto's staff who was enthusiastic about the plan for an attack on Pearl Harbor

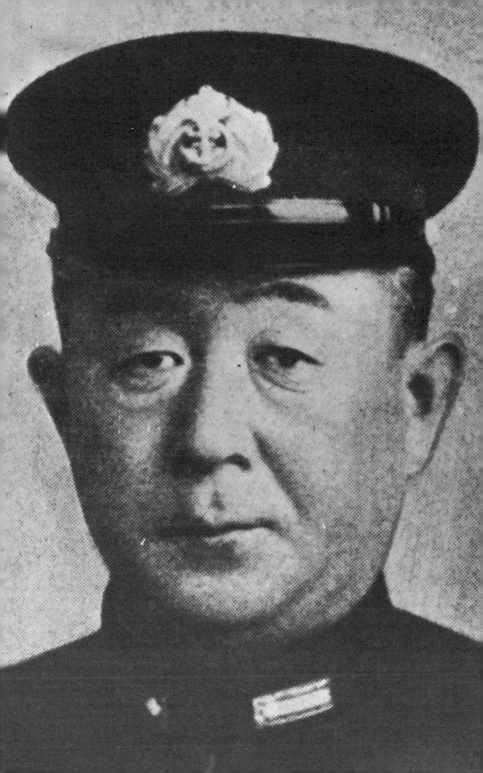

If the diplomats failed . . . the Imperial Navy was committed to an attack on Pearl Harbor

it had started. Soviet Russia had to be watched. As the political situation had deteriorated within the last couple of months, the Americans could be expected to be preparing to meet a surprise attack. And if the Americans had rumbled the possibility of Operation Z the Japanese could be sailing into a trap. High seas at that time of the year would make refuelling *en route* impossible. So the arguments continued, until Yamamoto rose and the conference was silenced. Slowly, sardonically, but with unmistakable determination, the commander-in-chief announced that he had listened with great interest. Some of the points that had been raised were relevant; he would take note of them. But having studied the strategic situation over a long period, he had concluded that Operation Z was essential to Japan's grand strategy. Therefore, he wanted to make it quite clear that while he, Yamamoto, was commander-in-chief of the Combined Fleet, the operation against Pearl Harbor would take place.

After this there could be no more arguing – in the fleet, anyway. Every

senior officer serving under Yamamoto's command now knew that if the diplomats failed to reach an understanding with the United States, and Yamamoto had his way, the Imperial Navy was committed to an attack on Pearl Harbor. But the naval hierarchy of the Naval General Staff was still opposed to Operation Z and when late in October the Naval General Staff sent him five detailed objections to his plan it seemed that Yamamoto was not going to get that sanction. Not for nothing was Yamamoto a good poker player however; an emissary, Captain Kameto Kuroshima, was sent to Tokyo with a letter and with firm instructions not to return without obtaining approval for Operation Z. In the letter, Yamamoto wrote: 'The presence of the US fleet in Hawaii is a dagger pointed at our throats. Should war be declared, the length and breadth of our southern operations would immediately be exposed to a serious threat on its flank.

'The Hawaii operation is absolutely indispensable. Unless it is carried out Admiral Yamamoto has no confidence that he can fulfill his assigned responsibility. The numerous difficulties of this operation do not make it impossible. Weather conditions worry us most but as there are seven days in a month when refuelling at sea is possible the chance of success is by no means small. If good fortune is bestowed upon us we will be assured of success.

'Should the Hawaii operation by chance end in failure, that would merely imply that fortune is not on our side. That should also be the time for definitely halting all operations . . .' The letter concluded: 'If this plan fails it will mean defeat in war.' When it was presented by Kuroshima to Captain Tomioka, head of the Operations Section, the latter was visibly disturbed. Yamamoto would never have expressed himself so forcefully if he were not completely confident of success. But Tomioka was not to be stampeded and the five standard objections to Operation Z were reiterated: – Success depended solely on surprise. It was a large scale operation employing about sixty ships. These ships would have to be dispatched a month before the outbreak of war and were likely to attract attention. The Intelligence networks of Britain, the United States and Russia were believed to have been extended. The Naval General Staff doubted if secrecy could be maintained.

They did not agree that the Americans would make straight for Japan at the outbreak of war. They estimated that they would first establish advance bases in the Marshall Islands and then attempt island - hopping strategy. This meant Operation Hawaii was not so vital that it must be executed regardless of risk. If it were not carried out the Japanese would have time to concentrate all their strength in a decisive engagement for which they had long trained. It would be wiser to seek this battle in familiar waters.

Almost all naval vessels participating in the Hawaii operation would have to be refuelled at sea *en route* – the destroyers at least twice. Weather statistics showed that on only seven days of the month were conditions suitable for refuelling at sea in the North Pacific. If refuelling proved impossible, Hawaii would fail and all ships involved would have been uselessly diverted from other planned operations. One hitch could lead to another. If refuelling at sea met with difficulties the radio would have to be used, forfeiting secrecy.

The Radio Intelligence section of the Naval General Staff knew that the American daily air patrol had been extended to 600 miles from Oahu. This meant the task force would probably be spotted by American planes. Since the carriers would have to sail to within 200 miles of Pearl Harbor before launching their attacks there was a considerable risk of a counter-attack.

Any hint that this plan was in operation must at once wreck the negotiations then going on between the United States and Japan.

Kuroshima rebutted the objections with Yamamoto's best arguments but he saw he was getting nowhere, and asked leave to telephone Yamamoto. When he came back from the telephone he said: 'The commander-in-chief insists on knowing whether the plan is adopted or not.' When a non-committal answer was made Kuroshima continued tersely, 'I have been ordered to tell you that if Admiral Yamamoto's plan is not adopted, then he can no longer continue as commander - in - chief of the Combined Fleet; that he will resign – and with him his entire staff.' This was an impressive threat with which the shaken Tomioka felt unable to cope, and Kuroshima was told to wait while the matter was referred higher. It was an emotional moment – the showdown. Yamamoto had thrown his own career into the balance and only the Chief-of-Staff could give the answer. Kuroshima waited tensely outside Nagano's office while the decision was taken. Then Nagano came out and putting his arm round Kuroshima said: 'I will approve the plan.' It was a reluctant capitulation but Yamamoto had won; Nagano was not prepared to contemplate Japan going to war without Yamamoto at the helm of the Combined Fleet.

The date was 3rd November 1941; thirty-five days remained before the attack.

Espionage activity on Oahu

Japanese interest in Pearl Harbor can be traced back to the annexing of the Hawaiian islands by the United States in 1898. For some time Hawaii had only slight military significance. But as the advent of the Americans had brought the United States 3,000 miles closer to their homeland the Japanese kept a wary eye on all military activity in the region, and when Pearl Harbor became a naval base they took an even greater interest. By 1932, the year in which President Hoover decided a major part of the United States fleet would be kept in Hawaiian waters because of events in Manchuria, a tenuous network of spies had already been established in Honolulu. As the population of Hawaii included a large number of Japanese immigrants who had gone there in search of legitimate work, the task of smuggling in and recruiting secret agents presented few difficulties. However, the American authorities knew what was going on and from 1903 had kept suspect lists of many Japanese residents.

Signal Intelligence collected by covert Japanese radio stations monitoring the radio traffic of the US Pacific and Atlantic fleets, together with information supplied by submarines sent to observe, at periscope depth, the Pacific fleet in its training areas, also contributed to the build-up of the picture Japanese Intelligence was forming of US activity in and around Hawaii. So too did information from the naval attachés in Washington, from passengers and crews of ships calling at Honolulu, from the representatives of commercial firms in the islands and reports from Japanese consulates. The latter studied the newspapers and listened to the local broadcasts, diligently collecting items of Intelligence interest to send back to Tokyo. There was nothing unusual or unacceptable about this. Most consulates and embassies are engaged in some collateral Intelligence activity, sending home periodical reports on what they have picked up. American consulates in Japan and East Asia were doing exactly the same as their Japanese counterparts in Honolulu and the West Coast of the United States. Indeed the information received from the American consuls in Saigon, Hainan, Canton and Tsingtao was of considerable value in charting Japan's march to war with the West.

Such 'legal' espionage sometimes yielded vital information; an excellent example of this is the report which reached Tokyo in 1940 to the effect that the American fleet had abandoned its anchorage off Lahaisin on the island of Maui. Over a period of three weeks this valuable strategic information was disclosed by one of Japan's consular agents in Honolulu, a Buddhist priest, who had observed that the ships were not returning to their usual anchorages. Getting this information had not necessitated his becoming involved in any suspicious activity: all he had to do was to watch. But such important information rarely becomes available by such simple means, and as the normal function of consuls and consular officials is not espionage, great care has to be taken not to jeopardise them by involvement in anything illegal. And in any country spying in the accepted sense of the word is always considered illegal. An illegal espionage ring may have links with the overt Intelligence set-up since a channel has to be available along which the illegal agents can pass the information they have gleaned. But often no such contact exists and more often than not the officials who run the legal system are unaware of any illegal network. Nor is it unknown for more than one spy network to be established, each working independently and ignorant of the existence of the other.

In 1941 a number of Japanese secret agents were working in and around Pearl Harbor. But Japan's spy network was neither so efficient nor so extensive as many people in America subsequently were led to believe. In the witch hunt which followed Pearl Harbor only about a dozen individuals who had been sent to Hawaii under false pretences and assumed names were found to have been actively engaged in espionage. Most of them appear to have been inferior spies at that. One, posing as a grocer, had been seen speaking authoritatively to senior officers of Japanese warships making courtesy visits to Honolulu; and judging by their respectful demeanour he was better known to them as something other than a mere tradesman. Another was the proprietor of the Venice café, a seedy night spot popular with American sailors because of its 'Go-go' girls. When his premises were searched after the attack on Pearl Harbor, this individual's office walls were found to be covered with autographed photographs of uniformed Japanese officers. Amongst them was one of the alleged restaurateur, in the full dress of an officer of the Imperial Navy. Yet another of the agents worked as a chemist at a brewery in Honolulu, and he was addicted to the bottle. In his cups he would boast to all and sundry that he was really not what he seemed but an officer of the Japanese navy on a secret assignment.

Operating on their own and with funds to buy secrets if the need arose, such agents were supposed to ferret out information not readily available to the 'legal' espionage system. But as there were few secrets in Hawaii whose discovery needed the efforts of trained spies, their contribution to Japanese Intelligence was infinitesimal. What was going on in Pearl Harbor could plainly be seen from the Aiea Heights, or from one of the private planes which could be hired at the nearby John Rodgers airport. Furthermore, by courtesy of the United States Navy, free sight-seeing tours of the harbour were generally available to all, and at the gate of the Naval Yard an old Japanese had been permitted to set up a stall. There it was possible to linger and enjoy a fine view of the inner harbour merely for the price of a soft drink. Thus it can be safely assumed that it was from overt observation and published information rather than the reports of under cover agents that Japanese Naval Intelligence had sifted and collated the material from which Yamamoto's file on Pearl Harbor had been compiled. After that an ingenious statistical study of the observations revealed that the movements of the American ships conformed to a pattern and a similar study had shown that American air patrols also behaved in a predictable fashion – never more than three at any one time covering a quadrant which extended to a maximum of 800 miles north and south of Oahu. Outside this area there was an unguarded sector through which it should be possible for Japanese planes to approach Honolulu without being intercepted.

Not included in either the 'legal' system or the spy network was one other Japanese undercover agent in Honolulu who deserves mention. This man, Otto Kuhn, was not a Japanese, but a German who had been recruited in Tokyo in 1936. Kuhn claimed to have been an officer in the Kaiser's navy during the First World War. This may have been true, but in effect he was little more than a beachcomber seeking an easy and lucrative way of life and ready to jump at a chance to go to Hawaii to live more or less idly at Japanese expense. Having convinced the Japanese Intelligence organisation that he could be useful, funds were made available through a German bank in Berlin. This money enabled him to pose as a retired gentleman of substance, and he and his wife Elfriede, who had been given a perfunctory training in the duties of a spy by the Germans, together with a son and daughter, set themselves up in a comfortable house just outside Honolulu. In the next three years Kuhn and Elfriede separately tried a number of business ventures but none were successful and it was only thanks to the Japanese funds at their disposal that they were able to continue living in comfort and style. So far he had not had to do any work for his benefactors; he had been planted in Honolulu to await an 'emergency'.

During the autumn of 1939, Otto Kuhn was visited by a certain Captain Ogawa, and his role as a 'sleeping' agent was confirmed. Kanji Ogawa was the 'spy master' for the Japanese Third Bureau's Section 5 (the Japanese Naval Intelligence department which specialised in America) and at this time he was on a tour of inspection of his organisation checking on its efficiency and state of readiness. In his early forties, Ogawa was one of the few officers of the Imperial Navy whose career had been devoted exclusively to Intelligence duties. Able and industrious, he had foreseen a future need for accurate Intelligence on Pearl Harbor. Kuhn appears to have impressed him and Ogawa is reported to have left Hawaii confident that the German would give good service when he was 'activated'. But the spy master

was less satisfied with what he saw of the man responsible for overt Intelligence on Honolulu. Gunji Kiichi, the Consul-General, was an old diplomat with a pronounced distaste for spies and spying—as the paucity of reports on matters of interest to Japanese Intelligence had shown already. Excusing himself on the grounds that it was of secondary importance, Kiichi had left the collection of Intelligence to Otagiro Okuda, his vice-consul. Okuda did not treat the responsibility lightly but he was far too preoccupied with routine chores to be able to give the time to it that Ogawa considered was necessary. On the staff of the consulate there was a professional Intelligence officer, but as he was supposed to be there specifically to watch the activities of Korean refugees in Hawaii, the Intelligence work was done by one of the consular secretaries.

Ogawa considered that improvements in the system would have to be preceded by the removal of Kiichi, and in October 1940 the old consul-general was recalled to Tokyo. In the absence of a replacement, Okuda, the vice-consul, was promoted acting consul-general, and as soon as he was free of Kiichi's inhibiting influence the scope of the consulate's legal espionage activities was widened. Surveillance of Pearl Harbor was stepped up, and to watch the activities of the Pacific Fleet in Pearl Harbor more closely the services of two of the local Japanese-Americans were enlisted. One was a young man called Richard Kotoshirodo but nicknamed 'Masayuki', who was already employed as a clerk at the consulate. Every week he would visit each of the vantage points above Pearl Harbor to see which ships were berthed and where. The other recruit was a shabby, middle-aged taxi-driver by the name of Yoshie Mikami. Known among the other taxi drivers as 'Johnny the Jap', Mikami had had no formal education. But somewhere or other he had acquired a profound knowledge of naval subjects, and as most of his fares were American sailors picked up at the main gate of the Navy Yard this

Bernhard Julius Otto Kuhn, Japan's 'sleeping agent' at Pearl Harbor

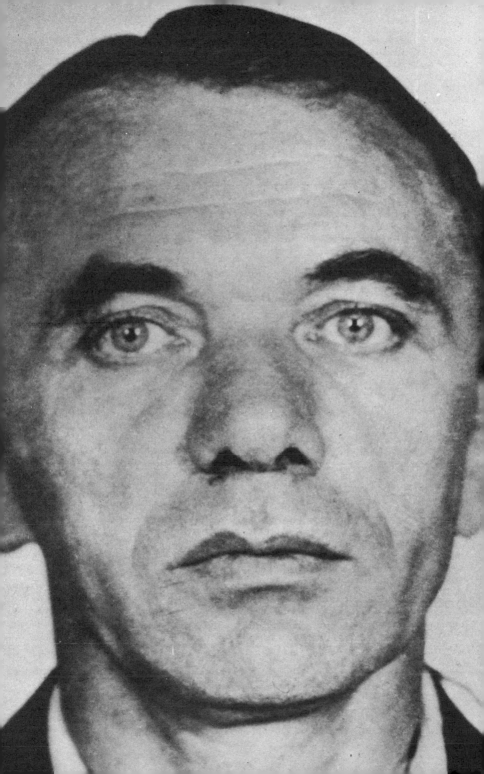

knowledge was invaluable. Driving them to places of relaxation downtown he would assiduously pump them for information on matters ranging from the thickness of their ships' armour to the calibre of the guns. In due course such technical data would be passed to the consulate-general for inclusion in the increased number of reports that Okuda was now sending back to Tokyo.

This, then, was the state of Japanese espionage in Hawaii when Yamamoto decided that he must know more about the American fleet based on Pearl Harbor and the defence arrangements at Oahu. On 5th February Ogawa was summoned to a conference on board the flagship *Nagato*, where he was told the outlines of Operation Z. Impressed by the importance of the projected operation, Ogawa saw clearly that the espionage cover of Hawaii would have to be augmented. But how? In the time available he could hardly hope to supplement his secret agents by planting others. On the other hand any radical changes in the numbers and personnel of the consul-general's staff in Honolulu might well attract attention and induce the Americans to tighten their security measures. One obvious course was to activate the 'sleeping' Kuhn. But the German was in financial difficulties and in the hope that he might be given more money had recently gone to Okuda in the consulate and suggested that he should 'emerge' and invigorate the Japanese Intelligence cover of Hawaii. Okuda, who till then had known nothing of Kuhn's dormant mission, had signalled Ogawa for confirmation of Kuhn's role and expressed an opinion to the effect that he thought the German was unreliable. In the circumstances Ogawa concluded that Kuhn was not fitted for the job he had in mind.

Ultimately it was decided that a trained English-speaking Intelligence officer who had specialised in the recognition of warships should be sent from Tokyo. The man concerned was twenty-eight years old Takeo Yoshikawa, a policeman's son who had retired from active service in the Imperial Navy during 1936 – ostensibly because it was discovered that he had tuberculosis. (After the war

Ogawa said that this was not an unusual arrangement for the recruiting of 'specialist' diplomats. Selected naval officers would be 'retired' for disciplinary or health reasons. Then, after a period of idleness to encourage a receptive frame of mind, they would be given jobs in the Japanese Foreign Office and sent where the naval background would fit them for Intelligence appointments.) As a civilian he had worked in the Naval Intelligence headquarters and whilst plotting the movements of ships of the Royal Navy in Asian waters, he had read everything possible about warships from such publications as *Jane's Fighting Ships* and *US Naval Institute Proceedings*. Then in 1940, after he had successfully taken an English language examination, Yoshikawa was officially taken on the strength of the Japanese Foreign Service as a diplomat. This was his cover, and his proficiency in ship recognition made him Ogawa's choice for the job in Hawaii.

At the same time as the decision to send Yoshikawa to Honolulu, Okawa asked the Foreign Ministry to appoint a new consul-general to take over from Okuda and fill the vacancy created by Kiichi's withdrawal. It was stipulated that whoever was chosen would have to be a man under whose sympathetic supervision the consulate in Honolulu could be developed into the focal point of espionage in Hawaii. After due deliberation, the Ministry decided that Nagao Kita, the consul-general in Canton, would be best suited to the post.

Born in 1895, Kita was a career diplomat who had spent most of his time at sensitive stations in which Naval Intelligence had a special interest: Amoy, Shanghai, Canton. A widower, fond of the ladies and *sake*, he was not a man to be trifled with, as may be judged by the fact that he had acquired the nickname 'the boss' during his tour of duty as consul-general in Shanghai. He arrived to take charge of the Japanese consulate in Honolulu on 14th March 1941, and twelve days later was followed by Yoshikawa. Carried on the first-class passenger list as 'Vice-Consul Tadashi Morimura', Yoshikawa had travelled in style aboard the liner

Nitta Maru, and as it appeared that he had paid a fare which amounted to a sum ten times the monthly salary of a probationery vice-consul this fact excited a good deal of comment among the rest of the staff of the Honolulu consulate-general. That no 'Tadashi Morimura' appeared in the Foreign Service List of diplomats and consuls was also strange, and when both Kita and Okuda evaded questions on the subject of their new colleague the aura of mystery was heightened.

Yoshikawa, or Morimura as he was now to be called, was met by Okuda and taken straight to Kita's office. There, behind locked doors the three men discussed their orders. In brief, Morimura's orders were to behave as a diplomat but submit weekly reports to Kita on the day-to-day readiness of the American fleet at the base; Okuda was to continue collecting information from the other overt sources and Kita was to collate all reports and send them on to Tokyo. That night at the *Shuncho-ro* (Spring Tide Restaurant) on the heights overlooking Pearl Harbor, the three men drank a toast to the success of their mission.

In appearance and deportment Yoshikawa did not match up to any of the conventional ideas of a master spy. Furthermore he lacked experience, although this could be counted an advantage as he had never appeared on any list of attachés to arouse the curiosity of US Intelligence agencies. In the consulate only Kita and Okuda knew what he was doing, and to the rest of the staff he was a brash, bibulous indolent, but handsome upstart with whom the consul-general was unusually tolerant. As soon as he had settled into a nominal job (he was officially registered with the US State Department as chancellor of the consulate) all he seemed concerned with was his own enjoyment. Within a few weeks Yoshikawa had made many friends, was well known in all the popular restaurants and night clubs, had taken up fencing at the Dai Nippon club, and between brief appearances in the office played golf. At night he stayed up late, drank heavily and flirted with the tea-house girls, many of whom he took round Pearl Harbor in a glass bottomed boat. The *Shuncho-ro* was one of his popular haunts, where on occasions when he appeared to have had too much *sake* the management would discreetly put him to bed in a room overlooking the harbour and Hickam Field. Few people who met the new vice-consul at this time credited him with much intelligence; most of them regarded him as an amiable buffoon.

Yoshikawa was playing his part well, for he was neither the simpleton nor the sybarite he pretended to be. Living constantly under the shadow of American counter-intelligence he had elected a casual approach to espionage and his role of playboy was his own shrewdly chosen cover. Everything he did served the purpose of his mission which he regarded fatalistically with the stoic submission of one who was merely doing his duty. On his own admission all he knew about Honolulu when he first arrived was that the Seaview Inn served an excellent balloon-fish soup. Within a fortnight he had familiarised himself with Oahu and in only a few months he had learned more about Pearl Harbor's defences than many Americans who had been stationed there for years had ever known.

To Honolulu's taxi drivers Yoshikawa was a boon. He could not drive himself and Kita had warned him that travelling in the same vehicle might make him conspicuous. For this reason he chose not to rely on Mikami to chauffeur him around. Much of his time was spent wandering around Oahu, often apparently quite aimlessly, taking buses and taxis, or walking if there was some special view he wanted to see. And it was views of Pearl Harbor and the airfields that interested him. From chosen vantage points he would gaze down on the harbour, checking the length of time necessary to get the fleet out, and how the ships moved, but never for more than a few minutes at any one spot. His aim was to avoid being caught and although he usually carried a camera on these expeditions, it was primarily as a tourist 'prop'. Nor did he take notes or make any sketches; what he saw on his wanderings was committed to memory, written up later and reported to Kita at night when the rest of the consulate staff were in bed.

That Yoshikawa was able to remain unsuspected is a tribute to his determination and forethought as well as his skill as an actor. There was no shortage of American counter-intelligence agencies in Hawaii and the Japanese consulate-general was under close surveillance. But never once was Yoshikawa ever suspected of being anything other than what he seemed – a rather dim junior official having a good time in Hawaii. Kuhn was on the suspect lists; so too was the grocer and the officer who posed as a chemist. But not Yoshikawa. Without fuss he maintained his exhausting 'observation' schedule until October 1941. And then the pace quickened.

On 23rd October the *Tatsuta Maru* arrived in Honolulu with two visitors from Japan who went straight to the consulate. One purported to be a Japanese Foreign Ministry official travelling on a diplomatic passport which disguised his true identity as a naval Intelligence officer; the other was a courier escorting the diplomatic bag. The Intelligence man had come to 'liquidate' the covert spy network, which he did by passing the word to the individuals concerned to wind up their affairs and make sure they were on a Japanese boat departing Honolulu on 1st November. The diplomatic bag contained a sealed envelope and 14,000 US dollars and in an accompanying note Kita was ordered to have this envelope and the money delivered to the 'sleeping' Kuhn. Kuhn's message was of course his 'activation' orders, and Kita decided that their delivery and the 14,000 dollars should be effected by Yoshikawa.

Conscious of the potential danger to his own cover, Yoshikawa did not relish the task. But to Kuhn the message came as the shock of his life. All he had wanted was easy money and the idea of becoming a star turn in some undefined catastrophic venture had no appeal. The message from Tokyo told him to devise a signalling system and be prepared for an important assignment. As Kuhn needed money, he decided he would have to obey. In the event the system devised by Kuhn was one of visual signals designed to warn off the Japanese fleet approaching Hawaii if the US fleet or parts of it had left Pearl Harbor in the days immediately preceding Sunday 7th December. The system was based on the information obtained by periscope observation by three submarines lurking off Oahu of three positions on shore. This information would then be radioed back to the fleet. House lights and a bonfire were to be used at night; during the day different shaped models were to be displayed. In the event the system was not needed and Kuhn was arrested.

On the morning of 1st November the *Taiyo Maru* docked at Honolulu. The usual carnival atmosphere and hula scenes were conspicuously absent, and the immigration officials took longer to inspect those who disembarked. Under the gathering war clouds, all Japanese shipping to the United States had been suspended. But this ship had been specially chartered to take home people who had been stranded in Japan or in Hawaii.

Unbeknown to the US authorities the voyage of the *Taiyo Maru* had been made for other than humanitarian reasons. From Japan she had charted the course of Admiral Yamamoto's task force, and disguised as stewards were two young officers of the Imperial Navy; one, Suguru Suzuki, was a member of Admiral Nagumo's staff; the other, Toshihide Maejima, was on the staff of Vice-Admiral Gunichi Mikawa, designated commander of the battleship and cruiser element of the task force. Instead of taking her regular course, on the instructions of the Japanese Naval General Staff the *Taiyo Maru* had followed a northern route between Midway and the Aleutians. During the crossing Suzuki and Maejima had recorded wind data and atmospheric pressures, and watched to see how many ships were encountered en route. Not one was sighted throughout the entire voyage.

The crew was allowed to go ashore on 2nd November and Suzuki went straight to the consulate to see Kita, who had been forewarned of his arrival

in a telegram from Ogawa. Kita was told that 'the day' was 'rapidly approaching'. Before leaving Suzuki also handed the consul-general a long list of urgent questions about the defences of Pearl Harbor. Yoshikawa was sent for, and that afternoon when Kita boarded the *Taiyo Maru* – ostensibly to supervise the repatriation of Japanese citizens in his role of consul-general – a package containing the answers to most of them was handed to Suzuki. It was the first question on the list that was most significant: 'Normally, on what day of the week would there be the most ships in Pearl Harbor?' 'Sunday', Yoshikawa had replied.

With the answers to the questions Yoshikawa had sent Suzuki a collection of other documents which included sketches of Pearl Harbor, a berthing plan and the layout at Hickam and Wheeler airfields. These were to prove invaluable to Yamamoto's pilots although it is probable

Emperor Hirohito presides over the Japanese Diet

that the most valuable acquisition was a set of postcards bought at one of the gift shops in Honolulu. Priced at only one dollar these gave an aerial panoramic view of Pearl Harbor, and less than five weeks later every Japanese pilot in the planes which attacked the base had a set of them in his cockpit. (The postcards had been photocopied and gridded into squares. Squares were allotted to aircraft and every pilot knew what ships he could expect to find in his own target area).

With Suzuki and Maejima aboard the *Taiyo Maru* sailed from Honolulu on 5th November. The extrovert ex-Lieutenant and the teutonic wastrel who remained behind still had a role to play. But with just over a month to go before the climactic act the espionage cover of the target area was virtually complete.

The sleeping giant

On 27th January 1941 (scarcely three days after Yamamoto had confided his scheme to Onishi) Dr Ricardo Rivera-Schreiber, Peru's envoy in Japan, called at the US Embassy to pass on a piece of information that had come to him at a diplomatic party. In a moment of indiscretion a Japanese interpreter had been heard to exclaim: 'The American fleet will vanish.' Gently questioned as to where it would disappear – San Diego? No. San Francisco? No. South Pacific? No. – the interpreter had recovered his pose, fallen silent and bowed himself out. Schreiber, pondering on the remark had eventually decided that only Pearl Harbor could have been meant. How the interpreter had got his information remains a mystery. It may have been an alcohol-inspired guess. But Schreiber's visit resulted in the sending of an immediate coded signal to the US State Department by the US ambassador to Japan, Mr Joseph Grew: 'A member of the Embassy was told by my Peruvian colleague that from many quarters, including a Japanese one, he had heard that a surprise mass attack on Pearl Harbor was planned by the Japanese military forces in case of 'trouble' between Japan and the United States; that the attack would involve the use of all the Japanese military facilities. My colleague said he was prompted to pass this on because it had come to him from many sources, although the plan seemed fantastic.' In Washington, Grew's dispatch was passed to the Naval Intelligence Division for 'information, evaluation and comment'. From there it was sent on 1st February to Admiral Kimmel, Commander-in-Chief of the US Pacific Fleet with the experts' comment: 'The Division of Naval Intelligence places no credence in these rumours. Based on known data regarding the present disposition and employment of Japanese naval and army forces, no move against Pearl Harbor appears imminent or planned for in the foreseeable future.'

In stilted and supercilious phrases the Intelligence experts agreed with the Peruvian Ambassador: the rumour was too fantastic to merit consideration.

Smiling deception . . . the Japanese Ambassador to Washington, Admiral Nomura (left) and the special envoy Kurugu leave the White House

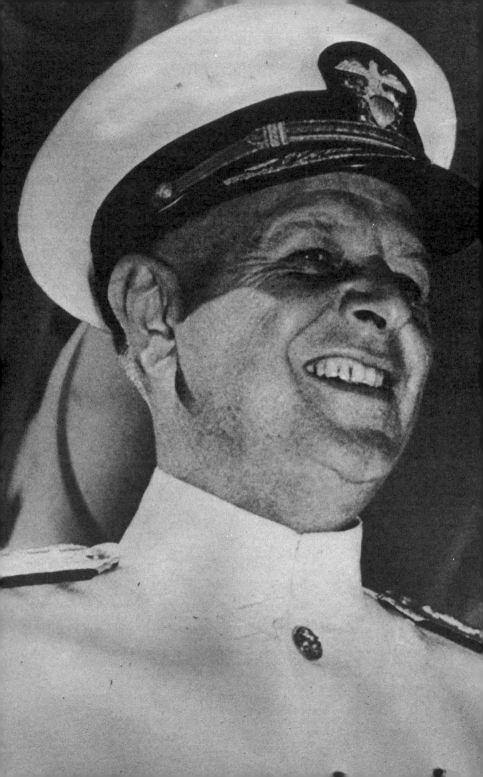

Independently, and without knowledge of Grew's dispatch, two officers in Hawaii had recently concluded that Pearl Harbor was by no means inviolate. On 16th January 1941 Rear Admiral Patrick L N Bellinger, Pearl Harbor's Air Defence Officer, had written to the Chief of Naval Operations expressing concern over the lack of modern aircraft, spare parts and personnel: '. . . I was surprised to find the Hawaiian Islands, an important naval advance outpost, was operating on a shoestring. The more I looked at it the thinner the shoestring appeared to be . . .' Two months later Bellinger and the commander of the US Army Air Force in Hawaii, Major-General Frederick L Martin, completed a prophetic joint appreciation, predicting the direction, strength, and strategy which would be used by an attacking Japanese force. Time would show that it was an accurate forecast.

Analysing probable Japanese strategy, Bellinger and Martin foresaw that the Japanese would probably use six aircraft carriers which would approach Oahu from the north, and that the most advantageous time to launch an air strike would be at dawn. If and when such an attack did take place, the Japanese would undoubtedly go to great lengths to achieve surprise. In the past, the two Americans pointed out, Japan had never preceded hostile action by a declaration of war. Nor was it safe to expect any prior warning from Us Intelligence; Japanese aircraft and Japanese submarines might well arrive in Hawaiian waters before the US Intelligence services had gleaned anything about their hostile intentions.

Until an act of war had been committed, the report continued, United States forces would probably take no offensive action if a Japanese task force was detected en route to Hawaii. On the other hand, if it was detected there would be time to disperse the ships in harbour and the defences of

Left: Admiral Husband E Kimmel, C-in-C of the United States Pacific Fleet in December 1941. *Below:* Rear-Admiral Patrick L Bellinger, Pearl Harbor's Air Defence Officer, who predicted the Japanese attack

Oahu would be ready. Forewarned would be forearmed and if the hypothetical task force knew that it had lost complete surprise it would be unlikely to risk an engagement. Thus, to forestall such an attack Bellinger and Martin recommended that air patrols should 'maintain a complete and thorough 360 degree search of the Hawaiian area during daylight'. To do so, the Hawaiian Air Force needed '180 B-17D-type aircraft or other four-engined bombers with equal operating range'. As the US Army Air Force did not have 180 Flying Fortresses and those that they did have were committed to the Philippines and the Atlantic, there were only twelve B-17s in Hawaii when the Japanese struck on 7th December.

The prophetic document reached Washington on 20th August, with a letter penned by General Martin. In it he wrote: 'Our most local enemy [Japan] can probably bring a maximum of six carriers against Oahu. The early morning attack is therefore the best plan of action open to them. They must also appreciate that to avoid detection by friendly surface vessels the most probable avenue of approach is due north.' This succinct summary could have been written by Yamamoto who at that very moment was putting the finishing touches to the plans for Operation Z.

In the mid 1930s the Japanese had devised a novel type of cipher equipment. Essentially this depended on a machine which was so original in its construction and so unique in the design of its cryptographic components that it seemed the closest human ingenuity could get to the ideal of an unbreakable cipher. By 1937 the majority of Japanese diplomatic dispatches were being encrypted on the new machine and for more than two years much of the information picked up by US listening posts monitoring Japanese radio traffic was of little value. With the sour smell of war already in the air the Americans concluded that national security depended on knowing what the Japanese were doing, and a small team of US cryptologists set about trying to unscramble the code. By the end of August 1940 they had broken it and the radio intercepts were intelligible once again. The diplomatic code was given the cover name 'Purple' and for the whole operation, involving the recording deciphering and translation, the melodramatic name 'Magic' was chosen

Undoubtedly breaking the code system was one of the most brilliant *coups* in the annals of Intelligence How it was done remains a mystery even to this day. The Japanese do not know and the handful of American officers who do will not say. Only one thing is certain. No Japanese officer gave away its secrets. Based as it was on the cipher used by the Imperial Navy, the cracking of the naval cipher may have led to the breaking of the diplomatic code. In this case it may well be that the British Admiralty supplied the knowhow. The Royal Navy, which had had a long association with the Imperial Navy, may have had priveleged information. A more unlikely theory, that the body of a Japanese naval officer carrying a code book was found, has also been suggested.

Whatever the means of breaking the code, the fact that the Americans could read top secret Japanese messages was worth more to them than a dozen Yoshikawas in Honolulu. Eventually it proved to be America's greatest single asset in fighting the Pacific war. Even before Pearl Harbor Yoshikawa's messages from Hawaii were all signalled in the Purple code and read by the Americans. Unfortunately Magic had not yet been developed into a perfect Intelligence tool. Its closely guarded intercepts were restricted to a narrow circle of highly placed recipients and generally regarded purely as *diplomatic* messages which would not necessarily reveal military intentions. At the same time the feeling that Japan was satisfactorily 'covered' bred a smug feeling of security. Assuming that Magic messages would serve prior notice of Japanese intensions, enabling the appropriate preventive of counter measures to be taken well in advance, President Roosevelt and his advisers came to rely on it. Napoleon is reputed to have said that 'a spy in the right place is worth 20,000 troops'. Japan had Yoshikawa at Pearl Har-

or; the United States did not have his equivalent in Tokyo, or at Kure and reliance on Magic as an instrument of warning became partly responsible for the complacency with which the American authorities approached the final crisis.

Both the US Navy and the US Army had special organisations to handle foreign radio intercepts. In the Naval Department the section that dealt with Magic was known as the Communications Security Unit was under the command of Captain Laurence ' Safford and had a staff of 300. In order to decode Purple quickly a special complicated cipher machine was needed and in 1941 only four were in existence. Two were in Washington – one with the Army and the other with the Communications Security Unit, one in the Philippines and one in London – given to Britain in return for the German (or perhaps Japanese) secret code at the outbreak of war. A fifth machine was being made for Hawaii but Yamamoto attacked before it was delivered.

If it could not be decoded on the spot, a radio message intercepted at one of the intercept stations spread out between Washington and the Philippines was sent back to Washington. Frequently messages went by airmail and sometimes this resulted in a long delay before they reached Washington. Translation from Japanese to English was also a bottleneck so that it sometimes took up to two months before the messages were available for distribution to the limited number of people on the intercept distribution list. Only the Secretary of War, Cordell Hull, the Chief of Staff, General Marshall, the Secretary of the Navy, Frank Knox, the Director of Military Intelligence, the Chief of Naval Operations, the Chief of War Plans Division, the Director of Naval Intelligence, and of course the President, were permitted to see the Purple messages. By restricting the number of people who knew that the diplomatic code had been broken there was less likelihood of the Japanese changing their cipher. In particular, Admiral Kimmel and the senior army officer on Oahu were deliberately denied any information culled from the intercepts and so far

as the Pearl Harbor authorities were concerned Magic did not exist.

Throughout the first nine months of 1941 the intercepted reports radioed by the Japanese consulate in Honolulu followed a consistent pattern which occasioned no concern in Washington. The routine movements of naval units had been recorded for some time but Yoshikawa and Kita had not yet got into their stride. On 24th September however a message from Tokyo completely changed the whole character of the consulate's reports. 'Tokyo to Consul General Honolulu, 24th September 1941.

Henceforth we would like to have you make reports concerning vessels along the following lines in so far as possible.

1. The waters of Pearl Harbor are to be divided roughly into five subareas . . .

Area A Waters between Ford Island and the Arsenal.

Area B Waters adjacent to the island south and west of Ford Island. This area is on the opposite side of the island from Area A.   .

Area C East Loch.

Area D Middle Loch.

Area E West Loch and the communicating water routes.

2. With regard to warships and aircraft carriers we would like to have you report those at anchor . . . tied up at wharves, buoys, and in dock. Designate types and classes briefly. If possible, we would like to have you make mention of the fact when there are two or more vessels alongside the same wharf.' (This message was decoded on 9th October 1941.)

In retrospect there could be nothing more significant than this message and the reports which followed. Before 24th January the routine Honolulu ship reports had merely kept Tokyo informed of the strength and composition of the US Pacific Fleet. After that date the Honolulu Consulate began to report the exact location of carriers, battleships and cruisers in Pearl Harbor as well as movements in and out of the base. Why? Because Tokyo needed the information to plan a surprise attack, and as the landlocked character of Pearl Harbor made only one form of attack possible, the rational explanation was that such an attack must come from the air.

Throughout November 1941, Magic's intercepts showed that Japanese interest in Pearl Harbor had intensified. On the 15th Honolulu was told to step up the frequency of its 'Ships in Harbour' reports to two a week. On the 29th Tokyo demanded reports even when there was no movement of ships. In several messages secrecy was stressed and there were frequent references to 29th November as a 'deadline' date. Some of the more important messages were not decoded in Washington until 4th and 5th December. Nevertheless there was still time to relay the significant revelations to Admiral Kimmel. Yet neither he, nor General Walter C Short, the Army commander in Hawaii, was given any hint of the existence of this irrefutable evidence of the forthcoming attack.

In Tokyo, the US Ambassador, Joseph Grew, was under no misapprehension about the way things were shaping. General Tojo's militaristic ambitions were common knowledge and tension had mounted quickly as soon as he had taken over from Konoye as the Prime Minister of a new government. In a broadcast on 2nd September, Colonel Mabuchi, Chief of the Army Press Section, denounced Britain and the United States for their 'unpardonable crimes' of attempting to strangle Japan by depriving her of her raw materials and freezing her assets. And, as the weeks slipped by Japanese newspapers became more and more provocative. America must cease giving aid to China, she must acknowledge Japan's leadership of the Co-Prosperity Sphere, she must lift the freezing order, she must recognise Manchuria. To warn the State Department against acceptance of any theory that the weakening and financial exhaustion of Japanese economic resources would bring about Japan's military collapse, Grew cabled a long despatch to Washington. In it he spoke of the

Secretary of State Cordell Hull, flanked by Admiral Nomura, the Japanese Ambassador to Washington (left) and Tokyo's special diplomatic agent Saburo Kurusu

possibility of Japan adopting measures with dramatic and dangerous suddenness which might make war with the United States inevitable: '. . . Japan will even risk national *hari kiri* rather than cede to foreign pressure . . .' A fortnight later Grew cabled again, calling attention to the necessity for vigilance against a sudden Japanese naval and military attack.

Meantime the Magic intercepts of diplomatic traffic to and from the Japanese Embassy in Washington and Tokyo indicated the obvious certainty with which the Japanese were moving towards their secret attack. In November 1940, Prince Konoye had appointed Admiral Kichisaburo Nomura as his 'ambassador of good will' to the United States. A good-natured, bumbling man of sixty-two, Nomura's only real qualification for the job was that he had known the President when Roosevelt was Assistant Secretary to the Navy during Nomura's time as naval attaché in Washington and was a friend of Admiral William W Pratt, former Chief of Naval Operations. Nomura had accepted, little realising what he was taking on, and as soon as the going got tough he requested permission to be relieved in order to return home. On 5th November Tojo offered America 'peace by negotiation' and, ostensibly to assist Nomura, an experienced diplomat, Saburo Kurusu, was flown to Washington.

Both the decision and choice of the new emissary astonished the State Department. Kurusu had been Japanese Ambassador in Germany at the time of the conclusion of the Tripartite Pact, and in fact it had been he who had signed it on behalf of Japan. It was true that a Magic intercept had shown that Nomura needed help, since he had told the Japanese Foreign Minister, Togo, that he could no longer bear up under the strain of 'all this deception'. But it seemed strange that Kurusu should be sent to replace the old Admiral if Japan was striving for a rapprochement. The mystery deepened when an intercept from Tokyo to the embassy – dated the very day of Kurusu's appointment – was translated. 'Because of various circum-

stances, it is absolutely necessary that all arrangements for the signing of this agreement [a reference to Tojo's proposal for peace, at the price of satisfying all Japan's ambitions] be completed by the *25th of this month* . . .' On 11th November, and again on the 15th and 16th, other messages from Tokyo had stressed the importance of the 25th, which was 'absolutely immovable . . . a definite deadline'. Furthermore, on 14th November an intercepted message from Tokyo to the Consul General in Hong Kong stated that if the Washington negotiations collapsed Japan would 'completely destroy British and American power in China'.

On 20th November Kurusu terminated his talks with the State Department and after a visit to the White House six days later he cabled Tokyo to the effect that his 'failure and humiliation' were 'complete'. From Tokyo came a commiserating reply: '. . . you two ambassadors have exerted superhuman efforts . . . therefore the negotiations will be *de facto* ruptured . . . But I do not wish you to give the impression that they are broken off . . .' The need to keep alive the appearance of continuing negotiations was stressed in another cable on 29th November and on 27th and 30th November in trans-Pacific telephone conversations between Kurusu and the Japanese Foreign Office.

Throughout the negotiations a deadline date had been stressed, after which 'things were automatically going to happen'. Yet automatic actions after the breakdown of such vital negotiations could only mean acts of war. Moreover, the dispatch to Hong Kong plainly stated that Japan had decided on war with the United States and Britain if the talks did collapse. That message was decoded on 26th November, the day that Cordell Hull handed Kurusu and Nomura the American note which effectively terminated the talks. Two days later any lingering doubts that diplomacy had completely failed should have been removed when the transcript of the telegram saying that the negotiations would be '. . . *de facto* ruptured' was received. Thereafter Tokyo, by repeatedly emphasising the importance of maintaining the appearance of continuing negotiations, implied that surprise was essential to those 'things which were automatically going to happen'. As history suggested that it was Japanese practice to start her wars with a surprise attack the writing was on the wall. Reviewed after the event it should have been obvious that Pearl Harbor would be the objective of that attack.

Were there any other alternatives? In fact Japan had only two sound objectives in the Pacific – the Pacific Fleet and the Panama Canal. And for her strategic purposes in the Western Pacific damage to the Panama Canal meant nothing in comparison to the crippling of the Pacific Fleet. With that fleet based on Pearl Harbor sound deduction should have reduced Japan's objectives in the Pacific to one.

The most drastic answer to a strained international relationship is a declaration of war. Short of war the most decisive action is the severence of diplomatic relations. In such circumstances ambassadors are recalled and their embassies are officially closed. Nevertheless some of the embassy staff may well remain in residence and the diplomatic inviolability of the closed embassies is fully respected. At the same time consulates normally continue to function because it has come to be accepted that they are not part of the diplomatic organisation. Consequently secret material in the embassies and consulates is inviolate during periods of ruptured diplomatic relations. If war is declared, however, the picture is very different. Embassies and consulates are seized immediately the declaration is made and their staffs are held in custody pending repatriation. Thus, when war seems imminent it is customary for ambassadors and consuls to make quite sure that nothing secret is likely to fall into enemy hands when their property is seized. Consequently orders to destroy codes, ciphers and secret correspondence can mean only one thing – that war is near.

To the Japanese the Purple code had the highest security rating and it seems that they never considered the possibility of it being compromised. Only their embassies and the more important consulates in such places as Manila, Singapore and Bataan had one of the special machines needed to encipher and decipher the code and secret communications with the other consulates were conducted in less secure codes. Bent on preserving the secrecy of their intentions but concerned about the security of the low grade codes of the consulates which were not equipped to deal with Purple, a special Winds code was devised. Two messages establishing this code were intercepted on the Magic net, and whether they could be interpreted as an announcement of the Japanese intention to go to war was subsequently the subject of much heated argument in the United States. One message from Tokyo to the Japanese Embassy in Washington dated 18th November, said: 'Regarding the broadcast of a special message in an emergency. In case of emergency (danger of cutting off our diplomatic relations) and the cutting off of international communications, the following warning will be added in the middle of the daily Japanese language short wave news broadcast.

1. In case of Japan-US relations in danger: *HIGASHI NO KAZE AME* (East Wind Rain).
2. Japan-USSR relations: *KITANO KAZE KUMORE* (North Wind Cloudy).
3. Japan-British relations: *NISHI NO KAZE HARE* (West Wind Clear).

This signal will be given in the middle and at the end as a weather forecast and each sentence will be repeated twice. When this is heard please destroy all code papers . . .'

A second message followed on 19th November: 'When our diplomatic relations are becoming dangerous we will add the following at the beginning and end of our general Intelligence broadcasts.

1. If it is Japan-US relations: '*Higashi*'.
2. Japan-Russian relations: '*Kita*'.
3. Japan-British relations (including Thailand, Malay and Netherlands East Indies): '*Nishi*'.

The above will be repeated five times and included at beginning and end. Relay to Rio de Janeiro, Buenos Aires, Mexico City, San Francisco.'

The first message was decoded on 28th November and the second on 26th November. Both had been given decrypting priority but as they had been garbled in transmission it took the American translater a long time to puzzle out what was really meant. As soon as their contents were known however, army and navy monitoring stations were ordered to keep a special listening watch on the Japanese broadcasts, and to telephone Washington immediately if any of the Winds code words were heard. At 8.30 am on the morning of 4th December Lieutenant-Commander A D Kramer, of the Communications Security Unit, walked into Captain Safford's office and said 'Here it is'. In his hand was a teletype message reporting that the Japanese phrase for East Wind Rain, meaning war or a break in diplomatic relations with America, had been used.

Whether this was an authentic message remains a mystery. (It may be coincidence that weather messages broadcast from Tokyo at 2200 hours GMT on 4th December reported: 'In Tokyo north wind slightly stronger, may become cloudy tomorrow, slightly cloudy and fine weather . . .' On 8th December, there can be little doubt that the winds code was used, when, in the middle of a news summary, the announcer broke off and said he would give a special weather forecast; 'West Wind Clear, West Wind Clear'. This, of course, signified a rupture in Japan's diplomatic relations with Britain. At the Congressional Investigation which followed Pearl Harbor, Kramer's teletype and a number of other documents connected with it could not be found. To those who believed that the President and some of his top-level colleagues knew that a Japanese attack was coming, and also where and when it was coming, their disappearance suggested that people in high places wished to destroy evidence of their knowledge.

Four other last-minute Magic signals deserve mention because they were recognised subsequently as a crucial tip-off. Their importance rests not so much on their contents, which made crystal clear the fact that Japan was going to war with America on 7th December, but at what time the privileged few looked at the messages and what decision they came to. The first

signal, which has become known as the pilot message, was decoded about 3 pm on 6th December – a Saturday. The second, known as the fourteen-part message – a long-winded presentation full of fighting words, giving Japanese views of their earnest efforts to secure peace in Asia despite obstructions by America and Britain – was processed about 9 pm that night. The third briefly told Nomura and Kurusu to present a note, already in their hands, to the State Department at 1 pm on the 7th. This message was picked up at 4.30 am and was quickly followed by a final code-destruction signal.

These messages should have completed the Intelligence picture. At about 3 pm Washington time on Saturday 6th December – twenty-one hours before the next sunrise in Hawaii – people in Washington knew that Japan had opted for war with the United States. Early on Sunday morning the deduction was that Japan would strike that day. But no word was sent to Hawaii, where the Pacific Fleet was enjoying a lotus-like weekend. Within twelve hours, President Roosevelt, long convinced that the United States must fight beside Britain in the battle for democracy, had solved his problem of how to persuade Congress to enact a declaration of war. The Japanese fired the first shots and on 7th December he was able to take a fully aroused nation into war.

The preparatory phase

While Yamamoto was putting the finishing touches to the plan for Operation Z the training of the carrier aircrews was intensified. This was his most urgent problem, and it was complicated by the need to maintain absolute secrecy. It was not possible to tell the airmen for what they were training. Yet different types of aircraft – high level bombers, torpedo bombers, dive bombers and fighters – had to be welded into an assault force capable of flying in formation to attack on a strict time schedule. If the operation was to be mounted towards the end of November there was little enough time to accomplish this. Fortunately the training area at Kagoshima was ideal for the purpose. With a 4,000 foot volcano in the bay representing Ford Island and Kagoshima city simulating the US Navy dockyard, it was shaped much like the projected target.

Farmers still complained that the constant din of engines caused their chickens to stop laying eggs, but by late September the local residents had come to accept what they now called the navy's aerial circus. Four times a day every pilot practised take-offs and landings from their carriers. Then the torpedo bombers would roar over the Shiro Mountain, dive low into the Iwasaki Valley and follow its winding course to the shore of the bay. There they would skim over the water releasing torpedoes. Meantime at other locations on Kyushu the dive bombers would be rehearsing their techniques – diving vertically from 5,000 feet to pull out steeply at the last possible moment. Until this time 2,000 feet had been the lowest acceptable release point for the bombs. But to ensure pin-point accuracy the pilots were told not to pull out of their dives until they had rocketed down to 1,500 feet. Constant practice and this lowered release-point altitude soon showed dividends, and the accuracy of the dive bombers improved. High level bombing was more difficult to improvise. The navy's airmen had a sorry record for high-level bombing even in China where air opposition was negligible. Yamamoto had criticised their performance and said that they were unlikely to register

Nakajima B5N2 (Allied code name 'Kate')
Engine: Nakajima *Sakae* 11, 1,000 hp at take off *Armament:* One 7.7mm
flexible machine gun in the rear cockpit and one 1,760 lbs torpedo or bomb
Speed: 235 mph at 9,850 feet *Climb:* 7 minutes 40 seconds to 9,850 feet *Ceiling:*
25,200 feet *Range:* 634 (normal) *Weight empty:* 4,830 lbs *Weight loaded:* 8,360 lbs
Span: 50 feet 11 inches *Length:* 33 feet 10 inches.

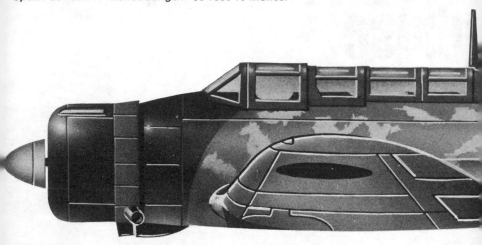

Aichi D3A1 (Allied code name 'Val')
Engine: Mitsubishi MK8 *Kinsei* 44, 1,000 hp *Armament:* Two 7.7mm machine guns
plus 683 lbs of bombs (550 lbs at Pearl Harbor) *Speed:* 242 mph t a7,610 feet
Ceiling: 31,200 feet *Range:* 1,130 miles *Weight empty:* 5,309 lbs *Weight loaded:*
8,041 lbs *Span:* 47 feet $1\frac{1}{3}$ inches *Length:* 33 feet $5\frac{1}{8}$ inches

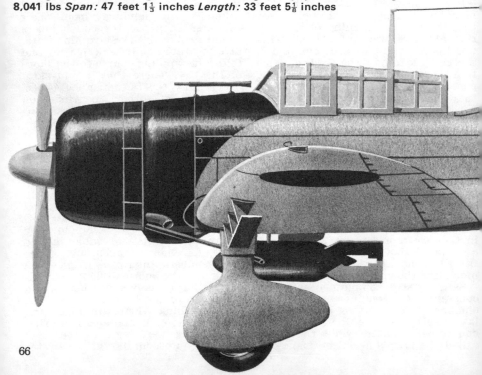

hits on a moving target such as a ship. But he believed that the ratio of bomb hits would improve if attacks were restricted to stationary targets. Basically the trouble was that Japanese bombsights were crude compared with those of the United States and Britain. Aiming depended solely on good eyesight and intuition. The latter could be developed by practice, however, and improved by putting the best bomb-aimers in the leading aircraft of each squadron. When these 'marksmen' pressed the release button the rest of their squadron would follow suit and, in theory, a pattern of bombs would straddle the target. At a bombing contest in October five high level bombers scored fifty per cent hits on a target ship moving on a zig-zag path at high speed. Against an anchored ship it was estimated that eighty per cent of their bombs would have scored hits.

Training the airmen was not the only problem that had to be faced. In March, Commander Genda had outlined the technical difficulties presented by the forthcoming attack. Unless the Pacific Fleet changed its ways, the American ships would be moored in pairs so that it would be impossible to reach the inner ships with torpedoes. Furthermore the anchorage was so narrow that the outer ships were only 1,600 feet from the far shore of the harbour and that shore was cluttered with high buildings, cranes and other dockyard obstructions. Another difficulty was due to Pearl Harbor being only forty feet deep. As Japanese torpedoes had been designed to drop at least seventy feet below the surface, new torpedoes would have to be manufactured which would not bury themselves harmlessly in the mud after release from the aircraft. Since the American battleships would be a priority target, armour piercing bombs capable of smashing through thick deck armour would also have to be produced, and tested to determine their most effective drop altitude.

Scientists and technicians worked feverishly to solve these problems. Making a new armour piercing bomb presented few difficulties, but perfecting a torpedo that would run shallow from the start was not so easy. After

seemingly endless experiments a design was settled on, which promised eighty per cent effectiveness when launched from altitude of twenty-five to fifty feet at a speed of not more than 150 knots. The decision to adopt this design came barely in time. Production started in mid September but the full complement of torpedoes was not ready when the first ships of the task force left Japan and the carrier *Akagi* had to wait until 18th November to collect the rest. Then when the *Akagi* arrived at the rendezvous with the rest of the fleet the remaining torpedoes were distributed to the other carriers.

Meanwhile the training of the torpedo-bomber pilots had continued. During October they had paraded to be told that their 'preliminary' training in a simulated fleet engagement at sea had been completed, and that the next phase would be advanced training in shallow-water torpedo attacks against anchored ships. Few of them saw any significance in the

new training programme, and most listened with sardonic amusement. Clearly stationary targets were of lesser importance than moving ones – simply because the latter were more difficult to hit. But the orders which followed soon put an end to any expectations of a lessening in the tempo of their training. For this form of attack they were expected to fly just above roof top height over Kagoshima city, and as soon as they had cleared the Yamagataya department store they would drop down to sixty-five feet, hold their aircraft on an even keel at a speed of 150 knots, and launch a dummy torpedo at a target only 1,600 feet from the shore of the bay. Such orders contravened almost every safety regulation the pilots had ever been taught. Travelling at 150 knots at only a few feet above sea-level, the slightest error of judgement would put their aircraft straight into the water. Nor was this all. After releasing their torpedoes they were expected to climb steeply, simul-

Commander Mitsuo Fuchida, responsible for the training of the air crews and leader of the first attack wave. Fuchida, wounded in the battle of Midway, survived the war and became a Protestant Minister

taneously making a sharp turn to the right. The whole exercise demanded a delicate balance between boldness and care.

Every day the torpedo bombers practised the new drill, while the citizens of Kagoshima grew accustomed to their city being buzzed. Every pilot made more than fifty practice flights, but in all the thousands that took place few accidents occurred.

To lead the air attack on the day, a man was needed who combined the abilities of a first class pilot with the usual qualities of leadership. On Genda's recommendation his friend and academy classmate Commander Mitsuo Fuchida was appointed. At twenty-nine, Fuchida had 3,000 flying hours to his credit and was a veteran of the war in China. Passionately keen on flying, hard-working and an extrovert, he was essentially a man of action. Genda, with whom he had to work closely, was first and foremost a staff officer. Genda did not suffer fools gladly and was impatient with those units were less able than his own. Fuchida, on the other had, had a tactful and magnetic personality to which men responded. Together Genda and Fuchida were ideal foils for each other and their relationship contributed much to the success of the training on which Operation Z ultimately relied. As Fuchida later described it: 'Genda wrote the script. My pilots and I produced it.'

The script called for split-second timing and pin-point accuracy on the day. This meant that each and every pilot must know exactly what he was expected to do, when and where. Recognising their own individual targets was obviously of the utmost importance. To this end a model of Pearl Harbor and the surrounding terrain was constructed and set up on board the carrier *Akagi* in late October. In groups, the pilots were summoned by Genda to the *Akagi*, told that an attack against Pearl Harbor was being prepared and shown the model. The purpose of practising mock attacks on stationary targets was now clear.

After reminding them that security was vital to the success of the operation, Genda explained the outlines of the plan so far as the pilots were concerned. Speaking in his customary expressionless monotone, he said there were two possibilities. If surprise were achieved torpedo bombers would strike first, followed closely by high-level bombers and lastly by dive bombers – which would best make their way through the smoke of earlier attacks. If surprise was lost there would be a 'storming assault' led by the fighters who would strive to gain control of the air over the targets before the bombers came in to do their work. Each method required a different approach and tactics, and the decision as to which type of attack would be used was bound to be difficult because the

choice would probably have to be made at 10,000 feet during the approach to Oahu. No one could fail to be impressed by Genda's brisk review of the essential details, and even the most fatalistic pilots confessed to feeling a cold chill of fear.

On 5th November, Yamamoto issued his 'Top Secret Operations Order No 1': 'The Japanese Empire will declare war on the United States, Great Britain and The Netherlands' read its preamble. 'War will be declared on X-Day. This order will become effective on Y-Day . . . In the East the American fleet will be destroyed and American lines of communication to the Orient will be cut . . .' An attack on Pearl Harbor had ceased to be a dream and had now become a reality. The only question now was when it would take place. To resolve this the Admiral sent for the fleet meteorologist, Commander Kanai Ota. The phase of the moon as well as the day of the week had to be considered, and Ota suggested 10th December as 'Y Day since that was the day when 'the dark of the moon would fall'. But 10th December in Japan would be 9th December in Hawaii – a Tuesday. And Yamamoto knew that the Pacific Fleet usually left Pearl Harbor on Mondays, returning after exercises on Fridays. As few ships were likely to be in Pearl Harbor on Tuesday, the nearest Sunday was chosen.

On 5th November also an Imperial conference was held in Tokyo. In a brief session two 'proposals' containing Japan's 'final terms' were approved. These were to be handed to the US State Department by Admiral Nomura and the special envoy Kurusu. Nobody present expected these terms to be acceptable to the Americans and the real purpose of the meeting was to instruct Japan's fighting forces 'to be ready to fight in the beginning of December'.

Everything was now set, and on 6th November there was a final dress rehearsal of the final phase of the projected operation. Six carriers and 350 aircraft staged a mock attack on a target 200 miles from the launching zone – duplicating the conditions, so far as it was possible, as they would be at Oahu. The exercise went well and although Yamamoto was too usy to watch it, his congratulatory signal flashed round the fleet: '*Kokegi ba, inigoto nari*' (The attack was splendid.) Next day the reluctant Admiral Nagumo, who still had hopes that something would transpire to cancel the operation, received 'Operations Order No 2' 'Y' Day would be 8th December 1941 – Sunday, 7th December in Hawaii. 'The task force, keeping its movements strictly secret, will assemble in Tankan Bay by 22nd November', ordered Yamamoto. (Tankan Bay, also called Hitokappu Bay and Tankappu-Wau, is in the Kuriles, the island chain to the north of Hokkaido, the most northerly of the Japanese Home Islands.)

At their bases the ships of the task force were stripped of unessential gear and made ready for action. Every item not considered essential to the operation was unloaded to make room for extra fuel, and with the exception of the carriers' flight decks all vacant space was stacked with oil drums. From his flagship, the carrier *Akagi*, anchored at Yokosuka in the Inland Sea, Nagumo directed that 'battle operations' should be completed by 9th November. On 11th November, Rear Admiral Natomi Ugaki, who had succeeded Fukudome as Chief of Staff to the Combined Fleet, delivered an impassionate address to flag officers of the task force. 'A gigantic fleet . . . has assembled at Pearl Harbor,' he said. 'This fleet will be utterly destroyed at one blow at the very beginning of hostilities. Should this plan [Operation Z] fail our navy will suffer the wretched fate of never being able to rise again. The success of a surprise attack on Pearl Harbor will prove to be the Waterloo of the war to follow. For this reason the Imperial Navy is massing the cream of its strength in ships and planes to insure success. It is clear that America's enormous heavy industry is being immediately converted to the manufacture of ships, planes and other war material. It will take several months for her manpower to be mobilised against us. If we ensure strategic supremacy at the very outset by attacking and seizing all key points at one blow while America is still unprepared we can swing the scales of later operations in our fav-

our.' Bowing ceremoniously he concluded: 'Heaven will bear witness to the righteousness of our struggle.'

Everybody concerned now operated on the timetable detailed in Yamamoto's plan. Between 18th and 20th November, a week before Nagumo's first carrier was due to sail, twenty-seven of Japan's big 'I' class submarines, in groups of three, set off from their bases at Kure and Yokosuka. Each of these great underwater cruisers had to be in position round Oahu before the air strike went in on Pearl Harbor. If Nagumo's attack failed and the American warships tried to slip out into the Pacific the submarines could still do great damage. If the need arose they would remain in Hawaiian waters to blockade Pearl Harbor, intercepting any American reinforcements and supplies coming from the west coast of Africa. The last five to leave carried Japan's secret weapon – five midget submarines, which were expected to slip into Pearl Harbor just before dawn on the morning of the attack and stay submerged throughout the air attack. Then, at sunset when the Americans would presume the action was over, they would surface and make a surprise attack. These tiny craft were derived from an idea for 'human torpedoes' suggested during the Russo-Japanese war. The original proposal was for a typical Japanese suicide weapon which would assure a hit by releasing a torpedo piloted by one man from a mother submarine. Initially, on the grounds that it was wasteful of trained personnel, the scheme was rejected. But when a method of recovering the submarines had been worked out Yamamoto was persuaded that the idea had merit and by 1941 twenty 'midgets' had been built. Displacing 46 tons, 78½ feet long and 6 feet in diameter, they had a cruising range of sixteen hours (175 miles) and could remain submerged for up to five hours. Five of them were allocated to the Pearl Harbor operation. Each was manned and was transported to the vicinity of Pearl Harbor clamped to the deck of an 'I' class mother ship, and was manned by two volunteers. None of these brave young men expected to return to Japan alive. Their mission

Japanese Type A Midget Submarine
Displacement: 46 tons (submerged) *Crew:* Two men *Dimensions:* 78½ feet by 6 feet by 6 feet *Engine:* One-shaft electric motor of 600 hp (submerged) *Speed:* 23/19 knots *Armament:* Two superimposed 18-inch torpedo tubes.

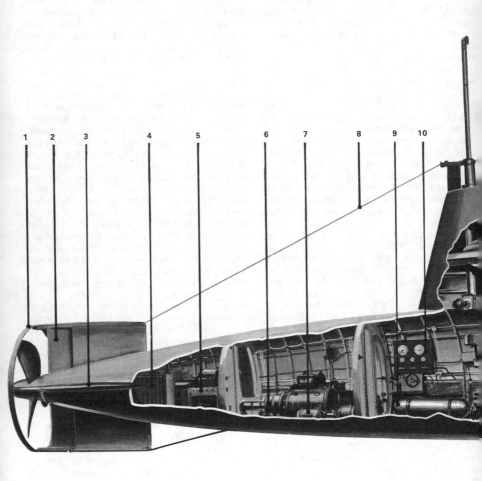

1 Propeller guard
2 Rudder
3 Aft hydro plane
4 Batteries
5 Gearbox and final drive

6 Electric motors
7 Generator
8 Aft jumper wire
9 Oxygen
10 Engine and speed instruments

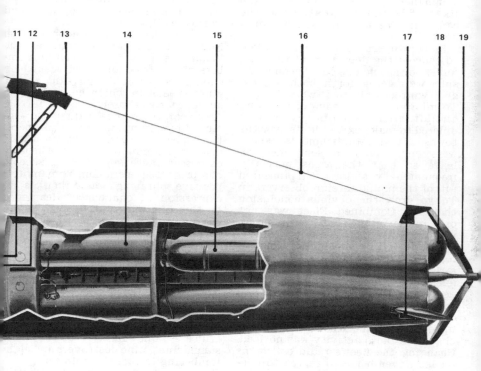

11 Coxswains seat
12 Wheel
13 Wire cutter
14 Torpedo tubes
15 Compressed air for launching torpedoes

16 Forward jumper wire
17 Forward hydroplane
18 Bow caps
19 Cap guards

called for the same spirit of self-sacrifice as that demanded by the *kamikaze* pilots towards the end of the war and they accepted their fate willingly. At a party on board the mother submarine *Katori* they asked the submarine fleet commander Admiral Mitsumi Shimuzu for permission to attack on their own initiative, rather than wait until sunset. 'Some of us will be so excited we might give the game away' said their leader. Shimuzu was reluctant to change the plan but in the end he agreed: each commander could attack when he liked; if he wanted to attack at the same time as the aircraft, he could do so.

Elaborate precautions were taken to conceal the departure of the task force. So that no one could deduce the ships were going north, both tropical and winter uniforms were issued. To minimise the exodus of so many aircraft, air force units nearby were ordered to make extra flights over the towns. Naval establishments ashore were encouraged to send men on leave so that the areas normally frequented by sailors still appeared full of them, and foreign observers in Tokyo drew the obvious conclusion that the Combined Fleet was not only in Japan but that half its crews were on leave.

When it left Japan ships of the task force had been ordered to keep a strict wireless silence. For the consequent diminution in radio traffic a deception plan had been arranged to take effect once Z force was under way. Dummy traffic had been built up for several weeks so that no abrupt change in radio activity was noticed. Changing the fleet's radio call signs on 1st November also served to confuse the US monitoring stations at a crucial juncture. The outcome was that most of the US Intelligence derived from radio traffic analysis during November proved fatally misleading. On 17th November, when Nagumo's fleet was en route to Tankkan Bay, Washington and Honolulu were advised that 'the Japanese carriers are mostly in the Kure-Sasebo area'. On 27th November, when the task force was well on its way to Hawaii, the carriers were placed 'in home waters'. After that US Intel-ligence had to admit that their monitoring teams had lost track of the main Japanese fleet. Asked by Admiral Kimmel where he thought it was at the end of November, the senior naval Intelligence officer at Pearl Harbor replied he 'thought it was in home waters', but he did not really know where it was. To Kimmel's quip 'Do you mean to say it could appear round Diamond Head and you wouldn't know?' 'I hope it would be sighted before that' was the answer. Since Nagumo's ships were then more than half way towards their objective, Yamamoto's deception had worked well.

During the late afternoon of 17th November Yamamoto boarded the *Akagi* to say goodbye to senior members of the task force and wish them good luck. After a short and rather glum speech in which he warned his audience to be prepared for 'terrific American resistance' Yamamoto concluded by saying: 'I *expect* this operation to be a success.' As, by ritualistic custom, a commander-in-chief usually expressed mere *hope* for the success of a projected operation, Yamamoto's positive phrasing was taken as an expression of confidence. Heartened by this his officers drank a toast to the coming battle and to the Emperor: '*Banzai! Banzai! Banzai!*'

That night those ships of the task force which had assembled in Saeki Bay blacked out, weighed anchor and slipped out to sea. Others left harbours up and down the coast to make their way to the rendezvous. In all there were thirty-one ships – six carriers, two battleships, two heavy cruisers, one light cruiser, three submarines, nine destroyers and eight lumbering tankers, as follows:

Carriers (Vice Admiral Chuichi Nagumo) *Akagi, Kaga, Soryu, Hiryu, Zuikaku, Shokaku.*
Support Force (Vice Admiral Gunichi Mikawa) Battleships: *Hiei, Kirishima.* Heavy Cruisers: *Tone, Chikuma.*
Screen (Rear Admiral Sentaro Omori. Light Cruiser: *Abukuma;* Destroyers *Tanikaze, Hamakaze, Urakaze, Asakaze, Kasumi, Arare, Kagero, Shiranuhi Akigumo.*
Supply Force (Captain of *Kyokuto Maru*) Tankers: *Kyokuto Maru, Kyokuyo Maru, Kenyo Maru, Kokuye*

Maru, Shinkoku Maru, Toho Maru, Toei Maru, Nippon Maru).

Three submarines had also gone ahead to reconnoitre the route in advance of Nagumo's task force and two destroyers *Akebono* and *Ushio* had been given the job of destroying the US air base at Midway Island simultaneously with the attack on Oahu. By 22nd November they were all in the bleak and craggy bight of Tankan Bay in Etorufu, the biggest of the Kuriles.

The Kuriles, the sixteen so-called 'smoking islands' because they are invariably shrouded in mist, do not appear in travel brochures. 1,000 miles north of Tokyo, surrounded by turbulent seas, only a few fishermen live here, eking out a bare living in a singularly unattractive region. For Operation Z, however, it was perfect, a buccaneer's dream of the ideal hideout. In complete isolation, with snow falling intermittently from grey winter skies, the most powerful fleet of aircraft carriers dropped anchor to await further orders.

On 22nd November Nagumo summoned his staff to the room aboard the *Akagi* where the model of Pearl Harbor had been set up. Here Lieutenant-Commander Suzuki, fresh back from his trip to Honolulu, was to brief them. Suzuki had nothing new to reveal, but as any first-hand information was avidly welcomed at this moment his audience was especially attentive. After speaking of the US fleet's habit of weekending in Pearl Harbor, he described the airfields and gave an estimate of American air strength on Oahu. (An overestimate in fact: Suzuki said there were 455 aircraft on Oahu; in the whole Hawaiian region there were only 231.) Nagumo said nothing until Suzuki had finished his report. But the series of questions which he fired at Suzuki gave the impression of a man whose mind was overfull of chronic fears. If Yamamoto was confident, Nagumo was certainly not. What about the possibility of being discovered en route to Oahu? Was it possible that the US fleet might not be in Pearl Harbor after all? What was the probability of retaliation after the strike? Reassurance on every point was not easy. Suzuki could only repeat what he had already told the Naval General Staff and Yamamoto in Tokyo: that the odds seemed to be in favour of the Japanese. And so far as the US carriers based on Pearl Harbor were concerned he could offer no reassurance. It was more than likely that these priority targets would not be caught in the attack, and it was this fact that worried Nagumo most. Early next morning, 23rd November, all commanding officers and key personnel from every ship in the task force swarmed aboard the *Akagi* to attend a special conference. There were still some who had not yet been let into the secret of their mission; indeed some naive individuals thought that they were on just another exercise. All such illusions were shattered when Nagumo told them why the force had been assembled in Tankan Bay. It was not absolutely certain that they would attack Pearl Harbor, he said, he was awaiting the final order from Tokyo. If the delicate negotiations being conducted in Washington were successful, the task force would return to Japan; but if they failed, the attack would take place. It would be a perilous operation but its success was imperative to Japan's war plans.

In Washington the diplomats already feared that the negotiations were doomed. The US military and naval chiefs of staff had advised President Roosevelt that war should be avoided for as long as possible. But all three knew that it could not long be delayed and according to the American Press 'every man from Rangoon to Honolulu was at battle stations'. Through Magic messages Washington knew that the Japanese Foreign Office had made 29th November the deadline, after which 'things automatically are going to happen'. The implication was that towards the end of November the first of a sequence of events would be initiated from which Japan would not turn back. And this could only mean one thing: war. In the event things started to happen a little sooner when, on 25th November, Yamamoto ordered Nagumo to sail for Hawaii.

The task force sails

The fateful voyage began in the grey pre-dawn of 26th November. When the ships weighed anchor the attack was not yet definite. But the final decision for war was made that day, and Yamamoto had anticipated it by twenty-four hours. (Prime Minister Tojo claimed later that he did not know the task force had sailed. It is possible since Tojo was an army man. But whether or not the navy had kept him informed, Tojo had already given the impression that Japanese belligerent action was imminent.) Kurusu and Nomura in Washington had presented Japan's final offer to Secretary of State Cordell Hull on 20th November. Japan would withdraw her troops from southern Indo-China if she was assured of free access to the raw materials and oil of the Dutch East Indies and of the resumption of American oil deliveries. Japan would remain in northern Indo-China and China, but the rest of south-east Asia would be regarded as a neutral zone; American support for China's Generalissimo Chiang Kai-shek must stop. Six days later Cordell Hull handed back the American reply. As interpreted by the Japanese i was nothing less than an ultimatum There were not even any concessions all the memorandum did was t reiterate an uncompromising atti tude. As a prerequisite to the liftin of sanctions the Japanese must with draw not only from Indo-China bu also from the whole of China. Wha America required them to do was t abandon everything they had gaine since January 1931. Without loss o face this could not even be considered The note clearly demonstrated, sai Tojo, that the Americans were 'in sincere'; Japan's very existence wa being threatened. The upshot wa that the Emperor was persuaded t empower the passing of laws to mee an emergency situation.

Under the Japanese constitutio the Emperor's permission was neede before hostilities could be opened And within the strictly circumscribe limits available to him Hirohito wa striving to find a formula by whic war with America could be avoide For months he had been anxious abou he way first Tojo and later the navy were behaving. On 29th November, with Nagumo's carriers three days out from Tankan Bay, a meeting at the Imperial Palace was called so that Tojo could be questioned about the crisis. (Protocol did not permit the Emperor himself taking part in the conference but his advisers expressed his reservations.) Tojo was adamant: war with America was unavoidable. In any case the chances of winning were better than the doubters might think. By knocking out the US Pacific Fleet and seizing south-east Asia Japan would hold a self-contained area in depth. The Americans would eventually see the hopelessness of continuing the fight and the conflict could be ended relatively quickly.

A more resolute Emperor might have intervened at this point. But Hirohito chose not to do so. He could exert influence on individual politicians but he could not dictate policy and by tradition his right of intervention was restricted to arbitration when there was disagreement on some vital issue in the cabinet. Possibly with the slender chance that this existed, he summoned Admiral Shimada, the Navy Minister, and Admiral Nagano, the Chief of Naval Staff, to a private audience the day before an Imperial Conference scheduled for 1st December. He had heard, he told them, that the Imperial Navy was not ready for war and so not entirely confident of its chances of success in war against the United States. This was a view which the Emperor's brother, Prince Takamatzu, a naval officer himself, had expressed. Was this true? If the two admirals sensed the meaning implicit in the Emperor's question they were now more anxious to retain the navy's initiative in a conflict that now seemed inevitable than hopeful of avoiding it. The navy they assured him was well prepared and 'reasonably' confident.

When the Imperial Conference was convened in the east wing of the palace next day, Tojo, to whom the list of the previous day's audience had been reported, made it clear that his government was determined to go to war with the United States in the following terms:

'It is clear we cannot gain our contentions by diplomatic means. On the other hand, the United States, Great Britain, the Netherlands and China have recently increased their economic and military pressure on us . . . Things having reached this point we have no recourse but to go to war against the United States, Great Britain and the Netherlands. . .'

His Majesty was rightly concerned, the Prime Minister said, but war was absolutely and urgently necessary. Every aspect had been considered and Japan would never be in a better position to win than she was now. In the unlikely event of the Americans deciding to concede Japan's demands for peace, he assured the Emperor, he was prepared to cancel the attack. Foreign Minister Shigenoru Togo then spoke confirming Tojo's view that diplomacy could go no further. Finally the two service chiefs (Sugiyama for the army and Nagano for the navy) followed with speeches in which they said that the nation's soldiers, sailors and airmen who were 'burning with desire to give their lives', awaited the Emperor's command.

The question facing the Emperor now was not whether there would be a war, but when hostilities would start. Togo, the Foreign Minister, had already clashed with Nagano on the timing of Operation Z and no doubt his concern had been passed on to Hirohito. Asked when he thought the war would start, because Japan would have to terminate diplomatic negotiations and make a formal declaration, Nagano had told Togo that a surprise attack had been planned. And Nagano's deputy, Vice-Admiral Ito, had added: 'We do not want to terminate negotiations until hostilities have begun – in order to achieve the maximum possible effect with the initial attack.' When the Imperial Conference had virtually agreed that war was unavoidable, the feasibility of continuing negotiations in Washington while Japan struck a devastating blow in the Pacific was debated. The first suggestion was that negotiations should be terminated at such a time as to give the Americans one and a half hours notice. Following further debate, however, it was decided that an hour and a half was too long and a

A Kate armed with torpedo takes off

dangerous interval, and should be reduced. Finally it was agreed that there should be 'at least half an hour' between the serving of a formal declaration of war in Washington and the bombing of Oahu. Uneasy with the outcome of the conference but constitutionally powerless, the Emperor accepted the decisions of his government and signed the rescript which irrevocably committed Japan to war. The exact time, according to the Secretary of the Cabinet Naoki Hoshino when Japan 'turned off the lights of peace in Asia' was twelve minutes past four in the afternoon.

At 10.30 am on 2nd December, when the cabinet in Tokyo ratified the decision taken the previous day, Nagumo's ships had been at sea for seven days. So far it had been an uneventful voyage. The weather was ideal: overcast skies, light winds and poor visibility. Cruising speed had been kept at twelve knots, which was the maximum pace of the slowest tankers. The carriers steamed in two parallel lines with the battleships *Kirishima* and *Hiei* astern while the heavy cruisers *Tone* and *Chikuma* kept station several miles away on either side. To ensure wireless silence, radio transmitters were sealed and most intership messages were passed by means of flags and signal lamps. Nevertheless some wireless communication had to take place, for it would have been sheer folly to expect the voyage for this armada of ships to be co-ordinated without it. Short wave signals from Japan could be picked up by the larger ships but for the small craft – more especially the low-lying submarines – this was impossible, because of their low aerials and the curvature of the earth. To solve this problem Nagumo's radio technicians had to resort to a subterfuge. High frequency (short wave) signals, picked up by one of the carriers, were re-transmitted simultaneously on a low frequency. These short range signals the smaller ships could intercept, and the hoax worked almost perfectly because none of the US monitoring stations was looking for a Japanese signal in the low frequency band. However, in war it is the unexpected that

counts (the overall success of Operation Z is one of the best illustrations of this maxim) and this tiny crack in radio security could have prejudiced the whole operation. On 29 November the luxury liner SS *Lurline*, flagship of the Natson Line en route from San Francisco to Honolulu, was three days out from Hawaii. Idly fiddling with the *Lurline's* extremely sensitive radio equipment, the radio officer, Second Officer Grogan – a forty-seven year old Irishman – picked up some faint signals which he could not identify. Grogan did not know it then, but he had stumbled on Nagumo's one security leak and for several days on he and his colleagues tracked the Japanese task force on its clandestine mission. Neither Grogan nor the *Lurline's* captain could solve the mystery. But intuitively they suspected the transmissions were from a source endeavouring to conceal its movements and concluded that they had detected a phantom force moving stealthily towards Hawaii. When the *Lurline* docked at Honolulu, a report to this effect was presented to the US naval authorities. Like the other bits of the Intelligence jigsaw no notice was taken. Nothing was done, and another warning was neglected.

Meanwhile, the Japanese fleet steamed relentlessly on towards its prey. Nagumo, weighed down by the suspense which had borne down on him from the moment the ships had left Tankan Bay, could not rid himself of the haunting fear of being spotted, and still hoped for a message from Tokyo cancelling the operation and recalling the fleet to base. Yet luck was on his side. The nearer the fleet got to Hawaii the worse became the gales and high seas. Men were washed overboard but there was no stopping to pick up the drowning sailors. Nor was there any slackening of speed when a thick fog descended to cloak the ships in eerie silence. The danger of collisions was accepted; in this fateful split-second operation the fleet had to keep to its time schedule and at least the fog provided cover. Below decks in the carriers the pilots pored over maps, studied scale models of their targets and discussed their mission over glasses of *sake*. Every few hours coded messages from the

Honolulu consulate relayed via Tokyo brought the latest Intelligence information of the activities in Pearl Harbor. In the radio rooms the Japanese kept a round the clock watch on transmission from the Hawaiian stations. Had the approach of their armada been detected? As the Honolulu stations continued to broadcast the usual peacetime programmes it seemed that the Americans did not suspect its existence.

The Americans, it seems, suspected nothing; their attention had been distracted. From Yokohama, the *Tatsuta Maru*, flagship of the NYK line, steamed out on 2nd December, purportedly bound for San Francisco. This luxury liner's plausible mission of 'exchanging American evacuees from the Orient for Japanese nationals in the United States' was widely publicised in the American press. The ship was scheduled to reach the United States on 14th December, and on 3rd December the *New York Times* took this 'as a token so far as Japan was concerned that nothing was likely to happen for some time'. But the voyage was a deceptive manoeuvre. Before the *Tatsuta Maru* sailed her master was handed a sealed envelope which was to be opened at midnight on 7th December. In it was an order to return to Japan, observing wireless silence on the way back.

Reports of Japanese convoys moving in the South Pacific and troop concentrations in Indo-China also served to turn American eyes away from Hawaii. On 28th November the *New York Times* speculated: 'It may be a Thailand Drive,' and in the issue which went to press on 1st December, *Time* reminded its readers that 'Envoy Kurusu and Ambassador Nomura' had been instructed by the Japanese Cabinet to continue the Washington talks. 'At least talking postponed war.' Events were moving with blurring speed and by the time this article was on the bookstalls it was obsolete.

At 5.30 pm on 2nd December (Japanese time) a signal from Yamamoto resolved Nagumo's lingering hopes that the attack would be called off. In cipher the cryptic message said *Niitaka-Yama Nabore* [Climb Mount

The battleship *Kirishima*

Niitaka], the code phrase announcing that negotiations had failed and war was certain. The number '1208' followed, and this meant that the date for the commencement of hostilities had been set for 8th December (Japanese time). In Honolulu, Otto Kuhn was trying out his signal system for Yoshikawa's approval, and in the Japanese Consulate-General's office Kita was burning his papers. Japanese consuls and ambassadors in other cities throughout south-east Asia were following suit.

In the task force itself tension was running high by this time. The fleet had just passed Midway, where the possibility of being discovered by an American patrol had been considered great. But the Japanese luck had held, and with subdued elation the sailors and airmen began their final preparations for battle.

In Tokyo there was one ticklish issue still to be settled. Under Article 1 of the Third Hague Convention, to which Japan was a signatory, a formal declaration of war was mandatory before hostilities commenced. The Emperor had insisted that Japan would abide by the letter of international law, and how to do so without alerting the United States had exercised many minds in the Japanese Foreign Office. Yamamoto protested vigorously that the delivery, prior to the attack being launched, of any diplomatic note containing the slightest hint of it, would prejudice the success of the strike. If the Emperor insisted on warning the enemy then the fleet had better be recalled. By Friday, 6th December (Japanese time), with telegrams pouring into the Foreign Office confirming the destruction of the secret codes at Consulates throughout south-east Asia and the United States, the question of a formal declaration of war had become a vital issue. The Navy maintained that no more than half an hour should elapse between delivery of the note which was to be interpreted as the notification of the existence of a state of war between Japan and the United States; Foreign Minister Togo was holding out for an interval of at least two hours. When a compromise was agreed the attack on Pearl Harbor was less than sixty hours

away. 'If the note is delivered at 1 pm Washington time Sunday afternoon, will there be a sufficient margin of time before the commencement of hostilities?' queried Togo. Speaking for the Naval General Staff and Yamamoto, Admiral Ito replied with emphasis: 'The margin of time will be *sufficient*.'

Nagumo was still forty-three hours from the point at which the carriers' aircraft would be launched when the submarine fleet arrived at its destination. Through heavy seas the twenty-seven 'I' class submarines had had a gruelling journey before they converged on Hawaii to take up their stations round Pearl Harbor. The nearest was only eight miles off Oahu, the farthest 100 miles away screening the surface fleet. They had been sent to reconnoitre radio information to the striking force if it appeared that it had been detected, and to join in the battle after the air attack. When they reached Hawaii they were to surface only at night; in daytime they would submerge to periscope depth. In five of them the crews of the midget submarines prepared for their sacrificial mission inside the harbour – scenting themselves with perfume as if for the ritualistic *hari-kiri* (nine of them did die. The sole survivor was Lieutenant Kazuo Sakamaki who was captured when his craft ran aground) that they might 'die gloriously, like cherry blossoms falling to the ground'.

For Nagumo the point of no return was reached at midnight on Friday 6th December (Japanese time). Apart from the stipulation that he should be ready to turn back if diplomatic negotiations in Washington proved successful, his orders permitted him to abandon the mission if they were discovered prior to 6th December. Everything seemed to indicate that the fleet had not been detected. There had been neither sight nor sound of aircraft; no ships had been seen by the scouting submarines and destroyers; no reports of anything untoward had reached him from the intelligence organisations; Honolulu radio continued to broadcast swing music. Only one issue darkened Nagumo's mood: the whereabouts of the US carriers. Originally Yamamoto had

Tatsuta Maru, **flagship of the NYK line, whose voyage in December 1941 was part of the elaborate Japanese deception plan**

hoped that up to six carriers would be trapped in Pearl Harbor. At mid-November his information was that the *Yorktown, Hornet, Lexington* and *Enterprise* were based on Hawaii and that the *Saratoga* was due to join them. Nagumo had been told that the *Saratoga* was still somewhere on the west coast of the United States, but not knowing the *Yorktown* and *Hornet* had been transferred to the Atlantic he could expect to find four carriers in Pearl Harbor – three anyway, if one was out on an exercise. Yet, according to a report sent by Yoshikawa on 5th December there were no carriers in Pearl Harbor. Where were they? Looking for him perhaps.

On Saturday the ships of the task force proper refuelled, and the tankers turned to make for a post-attack rendezvous. Meanwhile Yoshikawa was still doing his job, and during the morning Tokyo broadcast his latest information on Pearl Harbor. There were seven battleships and seven cruisers in harbour, he said. But no carriers. Five of the battleships had been in port for a week, two had returned the previous day. As it was a weekend none of the battleships were likely to put to sea before Monday, and they would be in harbour when the Japanese attacked. By the same reasoning the carrier *Lexington,* which had left Hawaii with five heavy cruisers on Friday, was unlikely to return. However, the cruiser escort to the *Enterprise,* which had left harbour a week before, had just returned, and there was a good chance that the carrier might enter the harbour that day. Of the *Yorktown* and *Hornet* there was no news. At 9 pm when Yoshikawa sent his final ship movement report, most of his deductions were confirmed: 'Ships at anchor at 1800 hrs: 9 battleships, 3 cruisers, 3 submarine tenders, 17 destroyers. In dock: 4 cruisers, 3 destroyers. All carriers and heavy cruisers at sea . . .' The count was not exact but the discrepancies were minor. Kimmel, as usual, had fetched most of his fleet back to harbour for the weekend. Only the carriers were missing. Perhaps it was fortunate for the gloomy

Nagumo that Japanese Intelligence did not know that the *Enterprise* was temptingly near Oahu. (Some of her aircraft flew from the carrier to Ford Island on Saturday to be caught by the Japanese next morning.)

Shortly after midday, with the task force little more than 500 miles from its target all hands were summoned on deck. Standing to attention, officers and men listened in tense silence while the Emperor's war decree was read, followed by a message from Yamamoto, echoing his hero Togo – and Nelson: 'The rise and fall of the Empire depends upon this battle. Everyone will do his duty to the utmost.' The battle-flag of the Rising Sun, which Togo had last run up on his flagship *Mikasa* in the Straits of Tsushima thirty-six years before, was then hoisted on the *Akagi*'s masthead. Patriotic speeches, interspersed with shouts of '*Banzai*' followed, and the ships, turning on a course which would take them due south, began their approach to the point from which the planes would take off. As discovery now would mean certain disaster the next few hours were ones of agonising strain. But fortune, it would seem, again favoured the Japanese. No American patrols were encountered and in a few hours when darkness cloaked the attackers the tension was lessened.

In the early hours of Sunday morning Tokyo relayed the last report from Hawaii. There were no carriers in Pearl Harbor, but the battleships were still there. No barrage balloons had been put up to screen the US fleet (as had been feared might have been the case); nor was there any evidence of torpedo nets protecting the battleships. Confirmation of the absence of the US carriers was bad news, but the rest was good. So too was the weather report on conditions around Oahu - obligingly broadcast every hour by the Americans themselves. Conditions for launching the aircraft were not too promising, but once the planes were in the air there should be no problem: 'Hawaii, you will be caught like a rat in a trap,' Admiral Matome Ugaki, Yamamoto's chief of staff confided to his diary.

The submarines were the first to go into action. Honolulu had gone to bed

discussing Christmas and President Roosevelt's appeal to Emperor Hirohito to avert war when the mother submarines launched their midget charges. About 3.45 am the officer on watch aboard the coastal minesweeper USS *Condor* - steaming slowly towards the Pearl Harbor boom behind another minesweeper, the USS *Antares* - spotted a suspicious looking object in the water ahead. The *Antares*, a target ship towing a cumbersome steel barge, was waiting for the boom to be lifted. Through glasses, the object bobbing in the water which appeared to be trailing the *Antares* was seen to be a tiny submarine with its conning tower awash, and as US submarines were prohibited from operating submerged in the area, this one clearly had no right to be there. The *Condor* signalled the destroyer *Ward*, which promptly moved in to attack, and as the destroyer bore down on the mysterious pigmy, an aircraft returning from a patrol

dropped a smoke bomb to mark its position. When *Ward* had narrowed the gap to a hundred yards she opened fire, missed, and dropped depth charges. It was now about 6.35 am, and with a murky dawn rising, the Pacific war had begun.

To admit the *Antares* and *Condor* into Pearl Harbor the harbour gates had been opened shortly before 6 am; they were not closed until 8.40 am. Although *Ward* promptly reported her encounter to the US naval headquarters, no one was particularly interested. Indeed people were still idly discussing it when the first of Nagumo's torpedo bombers screeched down towards Oahu. For nearly four hours the entrance to Pearl Harbor was open and two of the midgets managed to get through into the harbour. The success of the air strike subsequently obscured the unsuccessful efforts of Japan's submariners but as neither the midgets nor the bigger submarines succeeded in doing any damage, this

USS Enterprise

part of Operation Z can only be regarded as a fiasco.

Just before dawn, with the moon still intermittently concealed by clouds the surface fleet reached the take-off zone, 230 miles due north of Oahu. On the carriers' decks the planes were lined up for the take off, and their engines were being revved up as the fleet slackened speed and wallowed in the heavy seas. Nagumo, anxious still as to what would be found in Pearl Harbor, now decided to take a risk that had not been catered for in the plan. At 5 am a seaplane from each of the two cruisers *Chikuma* and *Tone* was catapulted off to reconnoitre the target area. An hour later these scouts had not reported back and the weather seemed to be deteriorating. Clearly it was going to take some time to get the strike force airborne, and the sooner it was launched the less likely the chances of losing

Banzai! Banzai!... The crew of one of the carriers cheer the aircraft taking off for Pearl Harbor

the vital element of surprise. But in deciding to launch the planes earlier than planned Nagumo ignored the split-second timing decided in Tokyo for the declaration of war to be served in Washington. Between the time Nomura and Kurusu presented their note to the State Department and the first bombs started to fall on Pearl Harbor there would be less than the thirty minutes interval prescribed by Tokyo. But to Nagumo this was a secondary consideration; his job now was to make sure the operation was a success. To Commander Fuchida, he gave the order: 'Take off according to plan.' Then turning to Commander Genda, he said: 'From this point the burden is on your shoulders.'

The crews were already standing by their planes, many of the pilots already wearing the white *hashimaki* – the cloth headbands which symbolised their readiness to die. The veterans, those with many flying hours behind them, felt more tense anticipation than fear. But, for the young officers who had barely completed their training, cold fear mingled with excitement. As they waited they had felt the pre-battle breakfast of rice balls and green tea coagulate in their stomachs. The day might bring a glorious victory, but they knew they might not live to enjoy it. But the die was cast. At 6 am precisely Fuchida roared off the flight deck of the *Akagi* into the dawn, as the assembled crew shouted three ceremonial *Banzais*. Behind him the rest of his squadron followed quickly. Within fifteen minutes forty-three fighters, forty-nine high-level bombers, fifty-one dive-bombers and forty torpedo-bombers had been safely launched. It was a record launching. In practice runs at Kyushu under good weather conditions the best launching time had never been less than twenty minutes. Now, not only had this time been cut, there had been only two casualties. One bomber had developed engine trouble and a fighter had plunged into the sea from the heaving deck of the *Hiryu*. As the attack force circled, swung into formation, and turned towards Oahu, Nagumo had every reason to feel satisfied; so far, his fears had proved unjustified.

Above: USS *Ward. Below left:* Minesweeper *Condor. Below:* Japanese aircraft revving up on the flight deck of the *Hiryu* before their mission on 7th December 1941

'To-to-to'

It was 6.15 am on 7th December in Hawaii. Honolulu was still sleeping on the Sunday that was to go down in history as the 'Day of Infamy'.

Almost as soon as Fuchida's first wave of 181 aircraft was in the air the crews on board the carriers were raising more aircraft up to the flight deck. In all there would be 353 aircraft taking part in the attack, the largest concentration of naval air power in the history of warfare up to that time. In addition to the attack force thirty-nine fighters provided an air umbrella above the fleet, and forty other aircraft were kept in reserve. As they watched the last of the aircraft speeding away, every man in the task force sensed with pride that this was an historic moment for Japan. Waiting in the *Akagi*'s operations room for the first news from Fuchida, Genda recorded that he experienced a resurgence of confidence. 'I found myself marvellously untroubled by any worry,' he said, 'with all care completely cleared away.' With rather less confidence, Yamamoto in the *Nagato* in the Inland Sea and with grim apprehension in Tokyo, the admirals of the

Naval General Staff also waited for news. Not only their careers but the fate of Japan depended upon Fuchida's air armada, now closing in on Pearl Harbor thousands of miles away.

The first message received was from the pilot of one of the two seaplanes Nagumo had dispatched an hour ahead of the first wave of attackers. Pearl Harbor was full of American ships, he reported, and there was no evidence of an alert. Then, at 7.49 am Fuchida's radio crackled '*To-To-To*' '*To*' is the first syllable of the Japanese word for 'charge', and it meant that the first wave had been committed to the attack. A few minutes later came the coded call that all was well, that complete surprise had been achieved, '*Tora, Tora, Tora*' [Tiger Tiger, Tiger] and it was promptly relayed by Nagumo to Japan. But by some wireless-wave freak Fuchida's low-powered transmission had already been picked up there. In Tokyo, and in the *Nagato*, the admirals listened with quiet satisfaction. The message was the curtain raiser for war across the Pacific and Indian Oceans. Immediately it was received Japanese aircraft prepared to attack targets over thousands of miles of front. Convoys of ships, filled with troops and waiting with steam up, set out on seven separate invasions of allied territory. And Japanese troops moved into position to attack a number of pre-planned objectives.

On the *Akagi*, Nagumo's chief of staff turned to his admiral and bowed ceremoniously. Back at Kure in the *Nagato*'s operations room Yamamoto took the news phlegmatically. His only reaction was to say to one of the staff officers: 'Check the time of the attack carefully. It is very important to know when it began, and it seems to have come earlier than we expected.' Yamamoto did not yet know that the Japanese ultimatum had not yet been delivered. Possibly because he suspected that this might be the case, he was anxious to establish the Imperial Navy's guiltlessness. In fact blame, if blame can be apportioned when the workings of a monstrous plot go awry, lay with the Japanese diplomatic service. Because of its ineptitude there had still been time for Pearl Harbor to be alerted; because of American ineptitude in Washington, occasioned perhaps by the fact that the crisis had been going on too long, the opportunity was missed. The fourteen-part Japanese memorandum which concluded: 'The Japanese government regrets to notify hereby the American government it cannot but consider it is impossible to reach an agreement in further negotiation' was not decoded and typed in the Japanese Embassy until later on the Sunday morning than had been planned. On the Magic net it had been picked up during the night and the American interceptions were five hours ahead of the Japanese in translating the message. Two hours before Fuchida signalled '*Tora-Tora-Tora*' the declaration of war could have been in the hands of the important people in Washington who had access to Purple messages. When they did see it, Fuchida's aircraft had already smashed the greater portion of the US Pacific fleet.

Back with Fuchida's air armada, the weather conditions improved steadily as the aircraft approached the target. Tuning his radio to the Honolulu radio station soon after 7.15 am Fuchida listened to the weather report with grim satisfaction: 'Partly cloudy, but clouds mostly over the mountains'. This was a promise of reasonable visibility with the advantage of cloud cover. He was not to be disappointed. The green island of Oahu woke to a beautiful sunny day; over Honolulu the sky was blue with a few scattered fleecy clouds. Banks of cumulus hung over the mountains and there was a fresh north wind down which the aircraft bearing the symbol of the Rising Sun came riding. For the Japanese it was perfect, especially as few of the officers and men of the US forces on Oahu were up to enjoy the beauty of the morning. Despite the growing tension with Japan, a relaxed way of life still pervaded Hawaii and there had been the usual social gatherings the previous night; for most people Sunday morning was a time to catch up on sleep. Only a handful of men had to be on duty.

But in the radar station of Opana, Privates Joseph Lockard and George Elliott plotted the course of an unidentified aircraft approaching Oahu which appeared on their screen at 6.45 am. Opana was one of five mobile detection stations set up at strategic points around the perimeter of Oahu. They were linked to an air warning information centre at Fort Shafter which kept a track of the plots picked up, and on any normal Sunday, Lockard and Elliott would have expected to plot about twenty-five control aircraft during the four hours they were on early morning duty. How they ran Opana was left more or less to the operators themselves; as it was a remote station, discipline was not strict, and the attitude towards what the radar screen showed was generally rather casual. Thus the presence of a solitary aircraft, which was actually one of Nagumo's two reconnaissance seaplanes, was not regarded as significant. When the radar screen showed what appeared to be a large number of aircraft, 130 miles away to the north, however, Lockard and Elliott decided to tell Fort Shafter. It was then seven o'clock and when they telephoned the air warning centre, the duty officer, a young and inexperienced lieutenant who was there purely for training,

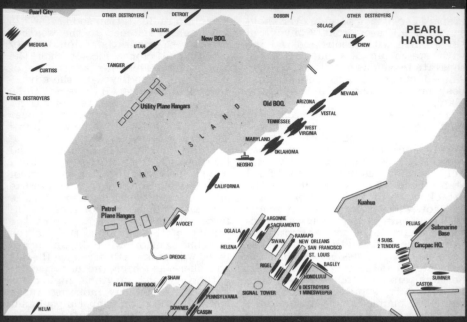

Above : Pearl Harbor on the morning of 7th December 1941
Below : The air attack plan

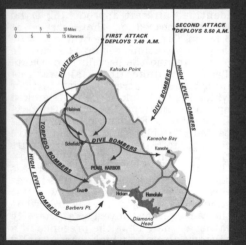

told them to 'forget it'. What they had seen must either be a patrol from Hickam Field or possibly a flight of B-17 Flying Fortresses which were due in from California. (And indeed twelve of these big bombers were approaching from the north-east at that very moment. But the aircraft that showed upon the Opana screen were a little less to the east, far more numerous and very much closer.) It was then about 7.15 am and Fuchida's powerful striking force was forty-five minutes away. There was still time for the island to be alerted, for the pilots to get into the air to face the invaders and for the sailors to man the ships' guns. It was the last chance for the Americans at Pearl Harbor, but when Opana's radar plot was dismissed as a flight of Flying Fortresses it had eluded them.

With a maximum speed of about 200 mph Fuchida's aircraft were primitive, slow and vulnerable by today's standards. But on that particular morning they were manned by what were probably the best-trained, most battleworthy naval pilots in the world. Fuchida, from the *Akagi*, was leading his own group of forty-nine bombers carrying 1,600-lb armour piercing bombs. Flying on his right, in command of forty 'Kate' torpedo-bombers, was Commander Shigeharu Murata from the *Akagi*. On Fuchida's left, commanding fifty-one 'Val' dive bombers, each carrying a 500-lb bomb, was Lieutenant-Commander Kuichi Takahashi, from the *Shikoku*. And flying above was a fighter escort of forty-three 'Zeros', commanded by Lieutenant-Commander Shigeru Itaya, also from the *Akagi*. All three men were veterans, their pilots the cream of Japan's fleet air arm; and like every one of their pilots fanatically committed to a Sunday morning of death and destruction. (Murata, Takahashi and Itaya were all killed during the war, but Fuchida survived to become a Protestant priest.)

The actual strike was scheduled to last ten minutes, and there were two plans for it. If it was evident that complete surprise had been attained, Murata's torpedo bombers were to go in first; Fuchida's bombers would follow, and Takahashi's dive bombers would deal with the Hickam Field and Ford Island air bases. If, however, it appeared that the Americans had been alerted, Takahashi's dive bombers would strike first and Fuchida's bombers would then bomb the anti-aircraft guns whose positions would be disclosed when Takahashi's dive bombers screamed down on to the base. Finally, in the ensuing confusion, the torpedo bombers would deal with the warships in the harbour. The operation was timed to begin at 7.55 am and the method would be signalled by Fuchida firing a flare. One flare denoted a surprise attack; two flares that the alternative second plan should be put into effect.

One hour and forty minutes after they had taken off from the carriers, Fuchida's pilots passed over the northern shoreline of Oahu; the time was 7.40 am. Ten thousand feet beneath them the island lay quiet and peaceful, bathed in the soft colour of an exceptionally beautiful dawn and cloaked in Sabbath peace. On the airfields, American fighters and bombers stood in neat rows like toys on a nursery floor; in the harbour not a trace of smoke came from the ships. Everyone appeared to be asleep, and in this atmosphere of soporific negligence, Fuchida reflected, never had the symbolic Rising Sun appeared more auspicious for Japan. 'Below me,' he wrote later, 'lay the whole US Pacific Fleet in a formation I would not have dared to dream of in my most optimistic dreams. I have seen all German ships assembled in Kiel harbour. I have also seen the French battleships in Brest. And finally I have seen our own warships assembled for review before the Emperor, but I have never seen ships, even in the deepest peace, anchored at a distance less than 500 to 1,000 yards from each other. A war fleet must always be on the alert since surprise attacks can never be fully ruled out. But this picture down there was hard to comprehend. Had these Americans never heard of Port Arthur?'

With the Honolulu radio still playing light music, Fuchida decided surprise was complete, and pushing back the canopy on his plane, he fired a single flare. Virtually the only thing that went wrong with the whole operation, and it was inconsequential,

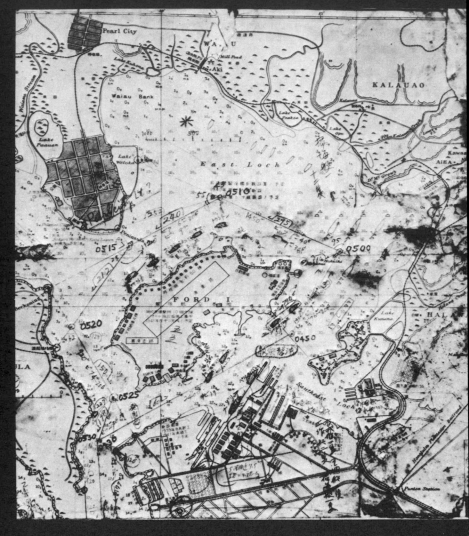

Above: Chart of Pearl Harbor taken from the Japanese midget submarine which ran aground after the attack. *Right:* Japanese plane over Pearl Harbor

A Kate over Wheeler Airfield. *Below:* Aircraft burning on Wheeler Airfield during the attack

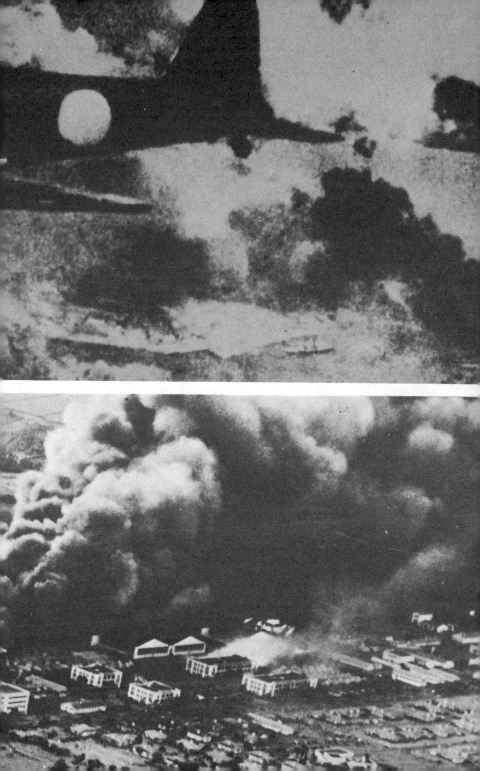

US plane on Wheeler Airfield after the first attack

Wrecked Flying Fortress on Hickam Field

now occurred. One of the fighter escort commanders, whose vision had been momentarily obscured by a cloud, failed to acknowledge the signal and Fuchida fired another flare to alert him. But two flares were the signal that surprise had not been achieved, an order that the bombing planes should attack first, eager to begin, Takahashi took his fifty-seven dive bombers up to 15,000 feet and split into two groups. Then, led by Takahashi, one group headed for Ford Island and Hickam Field, whilst the second led by Lieutenant Akira Sakamoto screeched down on the Wheeler air base. Murata, leading the torpedo bombers, knew that Takahashi had misread the signal. But as he had already descended almost to sea level to begin his attack on the unsuspecting battleships there was no choice open but for him to complete his part of the operation as quickly as possible. In the event, the fact that the dive bombers attacked slightly ahead of the torpedo bombers made no difference; surprise was so paralysing that there was little effective opposition to either. Fuchida, in the two minutes that remained after the flares had been fired and before the first bomb was dropped, sensed that this would be so. It was then that he ordered his radio operator to tap out the prearranged signal 'To-To-To'.

To the Japanese, the destruction of the American ability to hit back at their aerial armada was all important, and all fifty-one dive bombers had been assigned to this task. With nothing to oppose them in the air, the Zeros were able to join in by strafing the airfields behind Murata's aircraft. At Wheeler Field, which constituted the greatest potential menace, there were believed to be based more than fifty US fighters, P-40s and P-36s, and it was essential that they should be put out of action at the earliest possible moment. Ten foot high U-shaped earth bunkers had been erected to protect them but the fear of local sabotage, which was greater than any fear of attack from outside, nullified their use. To make it easier for an armed guard to keep

Wreckage at the Naval Air Station on Ford Island

an eye on them the fighters had been lined up in neat rows in front of their hangars. Sakamoto screamed down on them. The US aircraft were a gift target. A quarter of the base was disabled in the first assault and when Itaya's Zeros joined in, it was not long before it was like a raging inferno. Almost as soon as one of the US aircraft was hit, it turned into a fountain of flame, setting fire to the next, and the next, until the whole area in front of the hangars resembled a river of fire. Before the attack was over one third of the aircraft had been destroyed, the hangars ripped open, barrack blocks blasted and several hundred men killed and wounded. Wheeler Field fought back but the odds were too one-sided. When the bombers and fighters finally turned away Wheeler Field was a panorama of havoc and ruin. To the Japanese pilots, who that morning had expected to be flying to their doom, the whole operation had been easier than their practice runs.

Takahashi, leading the other group of dive bombers, had plunged down on Hickam Field a few minutes before the bombs started to fall on Wheeler. As at the latter base, their objective was the row of aircraft drawn up in orderly fashion in front of the hangars. Hickam was a bomber base and among the seventy parked bombers were twelve of the new Flying Fortresses. The maps of Hickam Field with which Takahashi's pilots had been provided proved hopelessly out of date. (In this Yoshikawa and his fellow agents seem to have slipped up.) But it did not deter the attackers and before Takahashi had finished most of the American bombers were no longer airworthy. It was the same story at the navy's air station at Kaneohe, a flying boat base on the east coast of Oahu, and the Marines' uncompleted air base at Ewa on Ford Island. All were within quick flying time of Pearl Harbor and at all of them every available US aircraft was grounded.

Ironically it fell to an officer on the staff of Admiral Bellinger, Commander Logan Ramsey, who with General Martin had complained so bitterly about the lack of preparedness nearly a year earlier, to broad-

Above: Commander Logan C Ramsey, the officer who broadcast the dramatic signal 'Air raid Pearl Harbor! This is no drill!' *Right:* the crew of the battleship *USS California* abandon ship as their vessel settles to the bottom

cast from Ford Island the dramatic signal: 'Air raid Pearl Harbor! This is no drill! This is no drill!' His broadcast was followed at 8 o'clock by a signal from Admiral Kimmel: 'This is NOT a drill.' Picked up by a US Naval Station in San Francisco Bay and relayed to Washington, where it was promptly passed to Navy Secretary, Frank Knox, Ramsey's news of the attack reached President Roosevelt and Cordell Hull just before two o'clock Washington time. At that very moment Nomura and Kurusu were outside Hull's office, waiting to deliver Japan's ultimatum. While they waited, the *raison d'être* for the attack was being realised. Murata's Kates, dividing into two groups, started their low fast run in toward the battleships shortly after eight o'clock. Every pilot had been allotted a separate target and in the first

Burning planes at the Kaneohe Bay Naval Air Station

The capsized *Oklahoma* in the foreground; *USS Maryland* behind

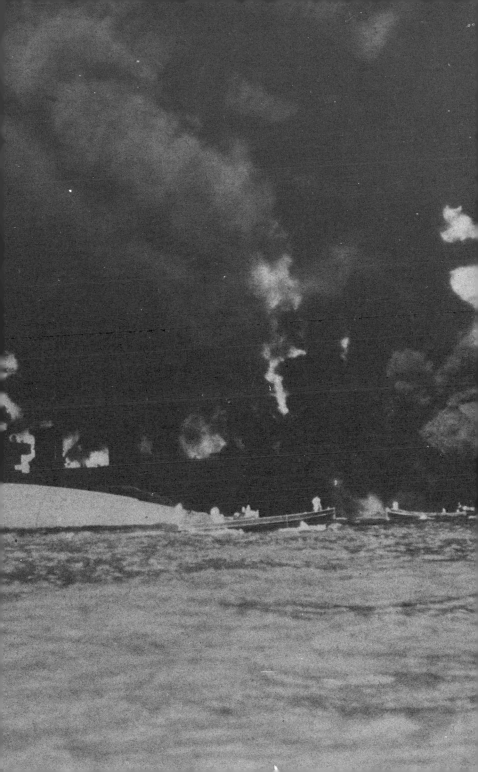

attack the *California, Oklahoma* and *West Virginia* were hit by one or more torpedoes. In a second attack, the cruiser *Helena* was struck and the minelayer *Ogala* moored alongside her capsized. In a third attack the cruiser *Raleigh* and the target ship *Utah* received two torpedoes apiece in quick succession. But even as the torpedo bombers zoomed in on their second run, some of the dive bombers, which had mistaken Fuchida's signal, were plummeting down on to the ships. Eight separate attacks were made from different points of the compass on the big battleships, and the pilots' aim was good. The result of this was catastrophic. With a deafening roar the *Arizona's* boilers and forward magazine blew up, huge fragments of steel debris rained down on the surrounding area, and burning oil from her tanks covered the water with flames. Massive explosions, the result of other attacks, rent the air, waterspouts foamed up and a thick pall of black smoke floated over Pearl Harbor; in the sea, wounded sailors splashed about feebly.

Circling above the harbour, Fuchida decided it was now time for his own high-level bombers to go into action and his forty-nine aircraft were formed into a single column, 600 feet apart. 'Not a single bomb is to be dropped carelessly,' he had told his pilots. 'If necessary make two, three or even four runs over the target.' (In the event, they followed his instructions faithfully and Fuchida himself made three runs over the *California* before he dropped his own bomb.) After passing over the harbour at 12,000 feet the long line of bombers wheeled to the right, and reversed its course for a second run by those who had waited. But by this time the Americans had begun to recover from their shock and, as the bombers turned, they were met by anti-aircraft fire from guns on ships and shore. Dark grey puffs of exploding shells bursting around the Japanese planes distracted some of the pilots and

Smoke coming from the *USS West Virginia* indicates where the ship suffered most damage. The *Tenessee's* superstructure can be seen in background

The light cruiser *USS Helena* (left) belches smoke. The capsized minelayer *Ogala* is in the foreground

many had to turn again to make another run before dropping their bombs. Two were shot down, and one, crippled by a direct hit, plunged down in a vain attempt to crash into his assigned target. Of his own bomb run Fuchida said 'I lay flat on the floor to watch the fall of the bombs . . . four bombs in perfect pattern plummeted like the devil's doom. The target was so far away that I wondered for a moment if they would reach it. The bombs grew smaller and smaller until I was holding my breath for fear of losing sight of them. I forgot everything in the thrill of watching them fall towards the target. They became small as poppy seeds and finally disappeared from my view just as tiny white spurts of smoke appeared on or near the ship . . .'

With his bombs gone, Fuchida climbed to 15,000 feet and continued to circle, trying to assess the damage. By now the anti-aircraft fire, especially from the ships and dockyard area, had become so strong that it was difficult to penetrate the veil

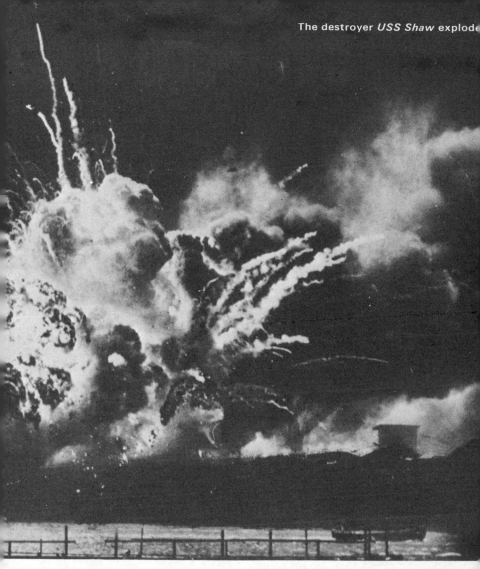

of smoke to see below. Neverthless, from what he could glimpse, it was clear that the harbour had been turned into a charnel house and that nearly all the battleships were sinking or on fire. At 8.40 am his radio operator reported that the second wave had crossed the eastern shore of Oahu and before he turned back towards the *Akagi* he saw the newly arrived bombers starting their attacks. According to the programme they were fifteen minutes late. Under the command of Lieutenant-Com-

mander Shigekazu Shimazaki of the *Zuikaku* the 170 aircraft involved had taken off while Fuchida was still on his way to Pearl Harbor, and they arrived before the first wave had finished, because of the number of passes Fuchida's ·bombers had had to make at their targets. Fuchida himself had planned to give target instructions to the incoming squadrons but this did not prove necessary and shortage of fuel precluded him staying for much longer.

Except for a few stragglers, the air-

*: A Val of the second wave of attackers. *Above:* Burning hangar at Naval Air Station, Ford Island. *Below:* Salvage work during the attack

craft of the first wave were on their way singly or in small groups to a rendezvous twenty miles north-west of Oahu by 8.45 am. There the bombers circled to pick up any fighters which, having low-powered radios and no navigators, would have difficulty in finding their own way back to the parent ships. Because it had been anticipated that American aircraft might follow them and so locate the task force, an elaborate deception plan had been arranged for the return trip. One group headed westwards from Oahu, to fly thirty miles before turning north again; another set a course which took them twenty miles due south before they swung back in a wide circle to fly north. Fuchida himself with insufficient fuel for any deceptive manoeuvring, after staying till the bitter end, flew straight back. And, before leaving the battle area, he flew round to make sure that there were no stray aircraft that had been left behind. Near the rendezvous point he picked up a couple of Zeros aimlessly circling, and these three planes were the last of the attackers to depart. Out at sea Nagumo had moved his carriers forty miles nearer Pearl Harbor since the morning. He had never intended to go closer than 200 miles from Oahu but he knew that an extra few miles might make a great difference to an aircraft short of fuel or crippled by enemy fire.

In the brief lull between the end of the attacks by the first wave and the onset of those of the second, the Americans had been feverishly preparing for the next blow. When Shimazaki's armada plunged down on them this frantic work had to stop. But the second wave pilots did not have such an easy time as their predecessors. The newly arrived dive bomber group, led by Lieutenant-Commander Takashigi Egusa, from the *Soryu*, consisted of eighty Val dive bombers whose original mission had been the destruction of the American carriers. Cheated of these, they had been diverted to attack those battleships which had escaped the first wave attack. Billowing smoke over the harbour made it difficult for the planes to pick out targets. But Egusa had decided that in the circumstances

it would be best to attack those ships which were putting up the fiercest barrage, and he led his squadrons straight down where the fire was thickest. Meanwhile Shimazaki's level bombers concentrated on Hickam Field, Ford Island and the Kaneohe airbase. Thirty-six Zeros had flown with the second wave to provide fighter cover but no American fighters came to meet them, and their commander, twenty-eight year old Lieutenant Fusata Iida, decided to lead them into a strafing attack on Kaneohe. A hard-drinking veteran who had survived three years of combat in China, this was Iida's last flight. American ground fire was much fiercer than he had anticipated and when his Zero was hit he put it into a vertical dive and crashed it into a flaming hangar. Before doing so it seems that he found time to signal his pilots to break off the attack whilst he died according to the *Bushido* code. A brother officer has recalled that his last advice to his men had been given only that morning: ·The most important thing for a soldier who is a true *Samurai* is his last determination. If for instance I should receive fatal damage to my fuel tank, I will aim my plane to effect the greatest destruction and, without thought of survival would throw myself into the target.' Iida thus died according to his principles and he was not the only Japanese airman to meet his death by such suicidal tactics. At Hickam Field at least one pilot followed his spectacular manner of leaving the world, a grim foreshadowing of the deadly Kamikaze attacks to appear later in the war.

Shimazaki's second attack, like that of Fuchida, lasted about an hour. Its casualties were higher, six fighters and fourteen dive bombers, but the least damaged battleships, and a number of cruisers and destroyers which had not so far been touched, were hit. The 29,000 ton battleship *Nevada* was trying to escape into the open sea and was pounced on as she limped towards the outer channel, with a torpedo hole the size of a

The Kamikaze spirit; when hit, Japanese pilots turned their aircraft into bombs

120

house gaping in her side. For the Japanese the sinking of this mass of steel to seal off Pearl Harbor was an opportunity too good to miss. Little wonder therefore that the dive bombers concentrated on the stricken vessel, and at least five hits and two near misses were scored. Somehow the *Nevada* remained afloat, however. Appreciating the danger, Rear-Admiral William Furlong sent two tugs to get her out of the channel and with the tugs' assistance she was deliberately grounded on the western side of the channel where she would not lock the Pacific fleet in or out of the harbour.

By 9.45 am the Japanese decided to retire. They withdrew, abandoning Oahu to a holocaust, and it was some time before the Americans realised that all was over. Jittery gunners shot down three of their own planes,

flying in from the *Enterprise* later that morning because they were thought to be Japanese.

Planes of Fuchida's first wave began to arrive back at the task force about ten o'clock, those of the second wave about two hours later. The weather had worsened and high seas combined with tricky winds made landing difficult. Some of the pilots, tense and tired, made bad landings. Yet the overall casualties were surprisingly even less than even Yamamoto had feared would be the case. Twenty-nine planes had been lost in actual combat, a few others at sea, or were so badly damaged in landing that they had to be pushed overboard in order to clear the carriers' decks for those coming in behind. Two bombers radioed the *Zuikaku* saying that they had lost their way and asking for the position of the task force. As the ships were

Above left: USS *Nevada* tries to escape to the open sea. On the tug
in the foreground the gun crews remain at the alert. *Above:* The *Nevada*
is beached on the western side of the channel out of Pearl Harbor

still maintaining a strict wireless
silence no reply was made. A final
message from the bombers said that
they were running out of fuel and
were going to crash into the sea.
Fuchida's report to Nagumo was:
'Four battleships definitely sunk, and
considerable damage inflicted on the
airfields.' 'In spite of growing opposition,' he said, 'I recommend another
attack'. To him all the evidence
pointed to an opportunity which
would never present itself again.
Except for their anti-aircraft guns,
the Americans had been stripped of
their ability to retaliate and this was
a time to 'mop up' the US base. The
planes were being rearmed and refuelled; most of the pilots were

anxious to go back and finish their
work of destruction. But Nagumo had
decided to call it a day. Somewhat
ponderously he announced that he had
concluded 'that anticipated results
have been achieved'. His statement
had a touch of finality that showed
the way his mind was working. He
had never relished the operation,
but he had been overruled. Yet he
had accomplished what had been
asked of him and got away with it.
He was not going to chance his luck.
   At 1.30 pm a signal flag was run up
at *Akagi's* masthead ordering the task
force to set a northerly course and
the carriers began to steam back as
swiftly as they had come. A golden
opportunity had been missed.

oahu under fire

Nobody on Oahu recorded a blow-by-blow account of the Japanese attack. The urgency of the moment precluded anything beyond fighting and clearing up the damage. Thus, the US record of the battle is in the stories of hundreds of men involved and in official statements, dictated while the harbour still bubbled with air escaping from the hulls of the sunken ships. As all historians are aware, such a record is never very accurate. (Some observers even reported seeing Messerschmitt fighters bearing the swastika emblem in action over Oahu on 7th December.) On 15th February 1942 in a report submitted to Navy Secretary Frank Knox it was pointed out that although there was agreement on all major events there were many conflicting statements in the individual accounts of the commanding officers of the ships in harbour regarding the attack. One thing everybody did agree on was that Operation Z was executed with remarkable skill. 'I must say . . . [it] . . . was a beautifully executed military manoeuvre' Admiral Kimmel testified. 'Leaving aside the unspeakable treachery of it, the Japanese did a fine job.'

Kimmel himself was up early on the morning of the attack. Abstemious by habit and energetic by nature, he had planned a game of golf with General Short, the Army Commander in Hawaii. After a strenuous week, which had reached a climax the day before with prolonged discussions on the disposition of the fleet (whether it should be kept in Pearl Harbor or sent to sea), the Commander-in-Chief felt in need of some relaxation. The admiral's Sunday morning golf never materialised. About 7.30 am, just as he was about to leave the house, the telephone rang. It was Commander Murphy, the headquarters duty officer, calling to report that the destroyer *Ward* had depth-charged a submarine near the Harbor boom. As Kimmel had ordered that all submerged submarine contacts near Pearl Harbor should be treated as hostile the *Ward's* commander had acted correctly. Nevertheless the incident would have to be investigated and Kimmel concluded that his presence was called for at fleet headquarters. Five minutes later, as he was about to leave, Murphy telephoned again; the *Ward* had got involved in another incident, with a sampan fishing well within restricted waters. In the middle of the conversation, a clerk dashed into Murphy's office shouting that Japanese planes were attacking Pearl Harbor and the duty officer relayed the news to Kimmel. Slamming down the receiver the admiral rushed outside to see for himself.

From his garden in Makalapa Heights, Kimmel stared aghast, as he watched Japanese aircraft zooming down on the naval base and listened to the crash of bombs and rattle of machine guns for what must have been the longest few minutes in his life. He could not have known it as he stood there, dazed with grief and in horrified disbelief that he was watching not only the death of his own fleet but the demise of the age of the battleship. The Japanese were demonstrating that this was the new era of naval air power. Ironically, it was because he had recognised the potential danger of the aeroplane to big ships that Kimmel had concluded it would be preferable to keep the Pacific fleet in port that weekend. When the carrier *Enterprise* steamed off to Wake Island to deliver planes and the *Lexington* to reinforce Midway, the fleet lost its air umbrella. Without any of its carriers it would be more vulnerable on the high seas than at its anchorages in Pearl Harbor where the ships would at least have the protection of the US Army land-based planes. Or so Kimmel believed.

By the time the admiral reached his headquarters at about 8.10 am, Fuchida's first wave of aircraft was approaching the climax of its attack. Torpedo bombers were skimming over Pearl Harbor towards the battleships, bombs were whistling down and exploding on the base, dive bombers were screaming in on their targets, there was the chatter and whine of machine gun bullets, the snarl from the engines of low-flying fighters seemingly strafing everything in sight, and there was an acrid smell of fire and smoke. All these sights, sounds and smells blended into a nerve-wracking blur of noise and chaos, and for most of the Americans caught in it the experience was momentarily paralysing. Kimmel himself could scarcely comprehend the disaster. Powerless to do anything about it, all he could do was to watch his ships being battered to impotency. From his office window, above the incessant crash of bombs, he could hear the anvil-clangs as Murata's lethal torpedoes plunged into the bowels of his ships, and see the rolling clouds of smoke from their burning.

Everybody was astonished by the effectiveness of the attack which was assumed to be coming from one or, at most, two carriers; on that Sunday morning even Kimmel would not have believed that a high proportion of Japan's total striking power was lurking over the horizon. The Imperial Navy was smaller than that of the United States, and although the latter had to be divided between two oceans, the combined sea power of the US Pacific fleet together with that of the British Commonwealth and the Netherlands should have been more than a match for Japan. But with the priceless advantage of surprise, Yamamoto had gambled with loaded dice. And, when news of the havoc in the harbour began to filter through to his headquarters, the complete destruction of the *Arizona*, the capsizing of the *Oklahoma* and the sinking of the *California*, Kimmel knew that Japan was, without doubt, the ruler of the Pacific, at least temporarily. He may have hoped for a chance of revenge. But in his heart he must have known that his professional career was finished when he rushed into the garden of his house and saw the host of aircraft bearing the Red Sun symbols on their wings.

There were many brave deeds performed that day, some of which were acknowledged in the award of fourteen Medals of Honor, fifty-three Navy Crosses, four Silver Stars and four Navy and Marine Corps medals. Boys became men and men became heroes in an hour. Once they had got over their surprise the Americans did their best to hit back. But unprepared, they were at a disadvantage. At Hickam Field, men ignored the strafing and worked furiously to disperse the aircraft. Some fell but others took their places. Two Japanese labourers helped a machine gunner to set up his gun and then fed it with

The *Arizona* after the explosion in her magazine

ammunition while he fired. Opposite the hangars one man kept up a steady stream of fire from a machine gun which he had set up in the nose of a bomber. When one of Itaya's Zeros turned it into a flaming death trap, the gunner did not even try to get out, and long after the flames had enveloped the nose of the plane, his red tracer bullets could be seen mounting skyward.

A Japanese view of Ford Island under attack

From Wheeler Field two young officers, Lieutenants Welch and Taylor, took off in their fighters and headed straight for a squadron of Japanese bombers. When they returned for refuelling Taylor had been wounded and one of Welch's machine guns had jammed; but between them they claimed to have accounted for three Japanese aircraft. Nor were Welch and Taylor alone. One or two other US aircraft managed to take off in the brief lull between the two waves of Japanese

attacks, and they too acquitted themselves well. The Flying Fortresses en route to Oahu from the United States arrived over Hickam Field in the middle of the attack. These were the B-17s whose expected arrival had caused the Opana radar plot to be ignored. The aircraft were not flying in formation and at the end of a fourteen-hour flight their crews were tired. Some had little fuel left; all were unarmed. Breaking through the clouds to approach Hickam Field they were set on by Zeros and when the airmen looked down they saw that their destination was an inferno. It is a tribute to the pilots that they were able to land their machines in such conditions. But all got down, most at Hickam, one at another airfield on Oahu's south-east coast and the other at an emergency landing strip on one of the island's north-west beaches.

Eighteen dive bombers from the *Enterprise* also arrived over Oahu during the attack, and thirteen of them successfully landed on the

In the middle of the cloud of smoke is the *USS Arizona*. The black puffs are anti-aircraft fire

Kaneohe Bay airfield, though not without considerable resistance from those manning guns on the ground. Nine of them which were still undamaged were refuelled and loaded with 500-lb bombs apiece,.and at 12.10 am sent out to try to find the Japanese fleet. Six B-17s had been sent off half an hour earlier to reconnoitre southwards, and they had found nothing. The *Enterprise's* aircraft went in the right direction but they saw nothing. Nobody thought to ask the radar air warning centre for information on the returning Japanese. Had they done so Yamamoto's fleet could have been located, for Opana had carefully plotted the planes returning to the task force.

As was explained in the previous chapter, what happened at the airfields could be considered incidental to the attack on the ships. When the *Arizona* blew up over a thousand dead men lay in her twisted wreck and burning oil from her fuel tanks cover-

ed the surface of the water around the stricken vessel. This, however, was a minor danger compared to the potential hazard contained in the fleet tanker *Neosho*, berthed near the *Maryland* and the *Oklahoma*. Full of high-octane aviation spirit, the *Neosho* was the first ship to get under way, and this action earned for her skipper, Commander John S Philipps, a well-deserved Navy Cross. In the jumbled confusion that followed the start of the raid, Philipps quickly saw the danger his ship represented. But while the *Neosho* was getting under way

the *Oklahoma* was under attack, and in a matter of minutes the battleship heeled gently over and capsised. The *Neosho* could now barely clear the battleship's exposed stern, and as she pulled out two torpedo planes came gliding in on a course that would launch their torpedoes against two of the other battleships. Diverted by the fire from the *Neosho's* guns their torpedoes narrowly missed the tanker. Meantime the *West Virginia*, which had been hit by several torpedoes, began to sink, the *Maryland* had been hit by a bomb which pene-

trated her deck and made an ugly hole in the port bow, the *California* was listing heavily to port, and the *Pennsylvania* was emitting dense volumes of oily smoke. All over the harbour men leapt from the decks of burning ships.

At the height of the air battle appeared another menace. One of the midget submarines surfaced about 700 yards from the seaplane tender *Curtiss* onto whose blazing deck one of the dive bombers had crashed. Guns aboard half a dozen vessels opened up when the stubby conning tower was spotted. But the submarine was not sunk by gunfire. Manoeuvring into position the destroyer *Monaghan* dropped two depth charges; then two more. With its crew of two inside, the battered silt-clogged hulk of this submarine was recovered during subsequent salvage operations. A new pier was being built in Pearl Harbor and after a military funeral service had been held over the midget, it was dropped into the concrete which now forms part of the permanent defences of the Pearl Harbor naval base. No sooner had this submarine been dealt with than another was reported to be heading for one of the US cruisers. Turning quickly, the *Monaghan* loosed two more depth charges and another oil slick darkened the sea; the second midget had been sunk.

Most of her crew were trapped in the overturned hull of the *Oklahoma*. More than 400 men died in her but thirty-two were rescued by workmen from the Navy Yard who cut through the battleship's armoured plates. Other men were imprisoned in the old *Utah*, an unarmed target ship, which also capsized. The task of drilling holes in the unarmoured sides of the *Utah* was easier than breaking through to the men of the *Oklahoma* but in both cases the work was hindby the continual strafing.

All the seven battleships moored along the southern edge of Ford Island were damaged in Fuchida's first wave attack. Four of them were moored

A picture taken just after the attack. The *West Virginia* and the *Pennsylvania* barely visible through the smoke of their destruction

together, two by two, and only the two inboard ships nearest the shore, the *Maryland* and *Tennessee*, escaped being torpedoed. All were hit by one or more bombs. The only battleship which got under way during the raid was the veteran *Nevada*, twenty-five years old and classed as 'over age'. Her anti-aircraft guns were among the first to be got into action but that did not deter the Japanese sufficiently to cause her to be left alone. Just before the *Arizona* blew up the *Nevada* was struck by a torpedo near the port bow and a bomb landed on her quarterdeck. When the *Arizona* exploded and the water round the *Nevada* was covered with flaming oil, the senior officer aboard decided that he would have a better chance of saving her if he could get her to open water. With some difficulty the ship was manoeuvred round the *Arizona* and the repair ship *Vestal*, which had been moored alongside the *Arizona* before the attack, and which was now covered with seething blazing fuel oil. Then, as has been recounted, as the *Nevada* moved slowly down the channel she became the number one target. Bomb after bomb exploded near her as the dive bombers screamed down from the sky to within a few hundred feet of her decks. Six of them struck home causing extensive damage and when she was run into shallow water she gradually settled down.

The 36,600 ton battleship USS *California*, moored near the *Nevada*, was hit by two torpedoes as soon as the attack started. With her lower deck flooded with fuel oil from ruptured oil tanks and gaping holes in her sides she began to settle. Like other ships which were later listed as sunk at their berths, the *California* was holed before the watertight doors could be closed. Later in the war American ships took worse poundings than most of those received at Pearl Harbor. But they were battle-ready and were able to move under their own power even with an entire section of the ship shot away. At Pearl Harbor none of the ships were ready, and so they sank. This was particularly true of the *California*. The battleships' guns went into action very soon after the attack started. But power was lost in the ship which meant that ammunition had to be

passed up to the guns by hand. Then, when blazing oil erupting from the holed fuel tanks ringed the ship, there seemed little likelihood of her being saved, and the order 'abandon ship' was given. In fact the *California* remained afloat for three days until she finally settled into the soft mud of the bottom, with only her upper works exposed. Like the *Nevada*, the *California* would live to fight again. With the exception of the *Arizona* and the *Oklahoma* this was equally true of every other ship damaged in the attack.

Of the other vessels in harbour at the time of the raid, the US Navy Department announced that three destroyers, *Cassin*, *Downes* and *Shaw*, had been lost. Later it turned out that none of them was 'lost' although all three were severely damaged. And had they not been immobilised in dry dock it is probable that they would have escaped with as little damage as the other destroyers in the harbour. Seven cruisers were in the harbour at the time of the attack, not nine, as the Japanese had believed. Three were attacked and the *Raleigh* came off worst. Moored north of Ford Island near the *Utah*, it is possible that some of Fuchida's pilots mistook her for a battleship. Torpedoed, dive-bombed and subjected to incessant strafing, the *Raleigh* did sink. But six months were to elapse before she was seaworthy. The *Helena*, which the Japanese mistook for the battleship *Pennsylvania*, received slightly less damage. (This was an understandable error; the *Helena* was at the berth usually occupied by the larger ship because the *Pennsylvania* was in dry dock. Less understandable was mistaking the *Ogala* for the *Arizona*.) The third cruiser to be damaged, the *Honolulu*, escaped with comparatively slight wounds, and she was able to put to sea in a month.

As could be expected, the damage was not confined to military targets, and there were over a hundred civilian casualties. Low flying Zeros machine gunned cars on the roads, and fragments of steel from spent anti-aircraft shells spattered the area. But the population behaved well and soldiers and civilians alike learned that day how narrow is the dividing line

The midget-submarine which was
grounded and captured

between them in wartime. Navy Yard workmen, many of them of mixed Oriental parentage, reported to volunteer their services. They were used to fight fires, clear bomb damage debris and even to pass ammunition. In the harbour non-combatant vessels also turned in a good account of themselves. Commercial tugs were used to move the repair ship *Vestal* from the *Arizona's* side, and to beach the battered *Nevada* after her run down the harbour. Even a refuse collection ship lumbered into action. She had no guns and was not armoured. But she did have pumps and this 'honey-barge', as such ships are called in the US Navy, pumped water on the burning oil round the stricken *West Virginia*.

Which American naval vessel was the first to fire as Fuchida's planes flew over was never established, although many ships laid claim to this dubious honour. The destroyers *Tucker*, *Bagley* and *Blue* were equally convinced, individually, that each had fired the first shot. So were the officers and men of the cruisers *Helena* and *Raleigh;* so too were the commanding officers of several smaller ships. However, if there was difficulty in deciding which ship fired first there was no doubt about the first encounter between individuals. To investigate a report that the wreckage of a Japanese plane was floating in the harbour the minelayer *Montgomery* sent its motor whaleboat. The aircraft was there and near one shattered wing the pilot was seen to be treading water. As the *Montgomery's* boat drew alongside the wreckage the Japanese was ordered to give himself up. There was no reaction beyond a sullen stare, and the order was repeated with pantomime gestures whilst the boat was manoeuvred closer. Just as the swimmer was about to be hauled aboard he was seen to drag a pistol from his jacket. However, before he had a chance to use it the coxswain of the boat shot him.

By Sunday afternoon Pearl Harbor was sure of only one thing – that the Japanese would be back from whereever they were. The 14-inch guns of the battleship *Pennsylvania* had been trained on the harbour mouth, and every sailor and dockyard worker who

was fit and well was struggling to get the undamaged ships ready for battle In the pier canteen a juke box repeatedly played 'I don't want to set the world on fire'; on the *Maryland* the band had been told to play martial music on the quarterdeck to improve morale. Fires were raging in and around the *West Virginia* and the twisted wreck of the *Arizona* was still burning. On the upturned *Oklahoma* salvage teams were cutting holes in her bottom to free men trapped in the hull. Other men were waging a losing fight to keep the *California* afloat. On shore the army was preparing to fight off an invasion and trigger happy sentries made movement a hazardous business anywhere on the island. Infantry, artillery and airforce men, who might have been better employed repairing damaged aircraft, were deploying at key points and digging slit trenches.

Fantastic rumours were rife. Japanese labourers were said to have cut directional arrows in the cane fields;

USS *Cassin* and *Dounes* in the dry dock

rs driven by local Japanese sabo-
urs were said to have deliberately
ocked the Honolulu-Pearl Harbor
ad. (All such acts of sabotage were
bsequently discounted by the local
BI.) The Japanese were said to be
nding at points on the coast, north,
uth, east and west. (With her other
mmitments Japan was in no
sition to mount an invasion of
awaii let alone supply and defend
) Shortly after midday, General
ort, who had set up his head-
arters in an ordnance storage
nnel, told the governor that the
land would have to be put under
artial law. Without the express
nsent of the President the governor
is unwilling to agree and at 12.40
n a telephone call was put through
Roosevelt. With Short saying that
could not afford to take chances,
e President agreed that martial law
uld be for the best.
It was about this time that a tele-
aph boy cycled up to Admiral
mmel's headquarters with a cable

from Washington. The message (which
had been sent to both Kimmel and
Short) had come by the 'fastest safe
means' through commercial channels
and it advised Kimmel that the
Japanese were presenting an ultimatum at 7.30 am Honolulu time. In
consequence the island defence forces
should be 'on the alert accordingly'.
As it did not carry any mark to
indicate that it was special or urgent,
this particular telegram had been in
one of the incoming pigeon holes at
the RCA office in Honolulu since
7.33 am. Delivery of all cables was
held up during the attack. The tele-
graph boy to hand it over was a
Japanese himself (an American but
a Japanese) and it took him nearly
four hours to get through the road
blocks to Kimmel's headquarters. By
the time it got to the Admiral its
interest was purely historical and
Kimmel hurled it into the waste-
paper basket.

ove: The capsized *Utah,* with the *Raleigh* in the background. *Below left:*
scue operations to release men trapped in the hull of *USS Arizona. Below:* The
ifornia still afloat but with a heavy list

Above: Wheeler Field, 7th December 1941. *Below:* Firefighters at work on the blazing *USS West Virginia*. *Right:* Kaneohe Bay Naval Air Station

Counting the Cost

In an attack lasting one hour and fifty minutes the Japanese won a stunning victory and inflicted a crushing blow on the United States Pacific Fleet. By noon on 7th December 1941· Pearl Harbor lay hidden, crippled under a heavy blanket of smoke. A survey of the damage showed that eight battleships, three cruisers, three destroyers and eight auxiliary craft, totalling 300,000 tons in all, had been immobilised. In addition, many of the installations at Hickam, Wheeler and other airfields had been destroyed; so too had ninety-six of the 231 aircraft of Hawaii's air force and only seven of the remainder were immediately airworthy. Finally, more than half the island's naval aircraft had also been knocked out. Casualties in the ships alone totalled 1763 officers and men, (not counting civilian casualties) and this figure, recorded immediately after the attack, was raised to 2335 by losses ashore. But this was death alone. Many officers and men were injured; many died, days and weeks later. Some recovered and went back to fight; others went home with their pensions and scars.

How could these terrible losses accounted for? *Surprise* was too sim an answer. By striking without wa ing and with 351 aircraft, the Japan overwhelmed the American forces Oahu. And in some ways the Am cans had made it easy. Nearly all battleships in the Pacific fleet w in the harbour; aircraft were bunc conveniently on the airfields. La of alertness was inexcusable, espe ally as such great progress had be made in the radar detection approaching aircraft since Admi Schofield's exercise in 1932. But m of the destruction was the dir result of the new technique of ae warfare so brilliantly exploited Yamamoto. The American admir did not believe that aircraft co launch torpedoes successfully in shallow waters of Pearl Harbor. T Japanese thought otherwise a

Above right: A Japanese officer, shot down in the attack, is buried with military honours near Kaneohe Bay. *Right:* USS California, with the Stars and Stripes still flying, is towed to drydock

proved their point. The American admirals also doubted whether bombs could penetrate massive deck armour; again the Japanese proved them to be wrong.

But the Japanese triumph was far from complete. In failing to destroy any of the American carriers they spared a weapon that was to be their undoing. What happened at Pearl Harbor led to the tearing up of all the old American plans. Some Americans, albeit in retrospect, considered that the Japanese not only sank a lot of 'obsolete scrap-iron' but also effectively torpedoed the old battleship theories. Because the *Enterprise*, *Lexington* and *Saratoga* escaped, *of necessity* the carrier replaced the battleship as the capital ship of the US Pacific Fleet. The carrier task force automatically became the principal naval weapon and almost at once the US Navy began to use it with great skill – at Coral Sea, Midway, Guadalcanal, Rabaul, the Marshalls and Truk. With the *Enterprise* it had been a close shave. Returning from Wake Island, she was saved only by a providential delay when her destroyer escort had trouble refuelling in the heavy seas. Even so she was only 200 miles off Oahu when Fuchida led in the first wave of attacking planes.

In failing to knock out the machine shops on Oahu the Japanese committed another blunder. These were to prove invaluable in repairing the stricken ships. Furthermore the oil tanks, in which was stored the life-blood of the fleet, were left intact. These tanks were above ground and thus highly vulnerable. Their loss might have driven back to America what remained of the US Fleet and the Japanese would then have had complete command of the Pacific for months. Those months might have made all the difference to the consolidation of Japan's position in south-east Asia. (In this respect luck could be said to have been on the side of the Americans. If the tanker *Neosho*, berthed near the fuel storage tanks on Ford Island, had been hit she would not only have made an inferno out of the four battleships moored nearby, *Maryland*, *Tennessee*, *Oklahoma* and *West Virginia*, but would probably have sent the storage tanks

up in flames. Intent on bigger game Fuchida's pilots allowed her to es cape.)

Although the damage might hav been worse than it was, the aeria attack must nevertheless be counte a Japanese success. (On the twenty fifth anniversary of Pearl Harbor th former Commander [then General Genda described the attack as 'a immortal success in the annals o military events in the world'. 'But he added, 'it was a great mistak politically because it eventually le to Japan's capitulation . . .') Th same could not be said of the rol played by their submarines. Th twenty-seven I-class and five midge submarines positioned round Oah failed utterly in their mission. Th midgets did not finish off any wounde

The body of a Japanese aviator

ships inside the harbour, nor did the big vessels sink the American ships which left it. The returning *Enterprise* and her three escorting cruisers offered especially tempting targets but it seems that the Japanese submarines were neither so well trained nor as aggressive as Fuchida's airmen. One I-class submarine and four of the midgets were sunk whilst the commander of a fifth midget grounded his craft and surrendered. (Only the nine men who lost their lives in the five midget submarines were honoured. Posthumously decorated and promoted two ranks, they were canonised as national heroes.) Thus this phase of Operation Z must be dubbed a fiasco. As a result the Japanese submarine service lost face and it was denied the funds which might

have helped it to develop. Later in the war many of the submarines were reduced to the role of supply ships to Japanese garrisons cut off in the Solomon islands.

When the super-cautious Nagumo decided that the object of the operation had been achieved, he is reputed to have quoted a Japanese proverb '*Yudan Kaiteki*' (Carelessness is the greatest enemy). Once the job was done his concern was to get back to Japan with his fleet intact. Part of Nagumo's caution stemmed from the fact that Japan could not afford to lose ships. The Americans could build others but Japan's limited industrial capacity was restricted by shortage of strategic materials and scarcity of

145

technicians. She was fighting a poor man's war and just could not afford to trade blow for blow with the American industrial colossus. According to Japanese Intelligence the Americans still had a large number of bombers in operational condition and to Nagumo it was foolhardy to remain within range of American land-based aircraft. Fuchida, incensed by his commander's prudence, never ceased to lament the decision not to allow his pilots another strike. 'Had we knocked out Pearl Harbor and destroyed either the *Enterprise* or *Lexington* or both,' he said in retrospect, 'the war in the Pacific would have been vastly different.' Many of the American admirals have agreed with him. Admiral Nimitz, who succeeded Kimmel as Commander-in-Chief of the Pacific Fleet, wrote: 'Future students of our naval war in the Pacific will inevitably conclude that the Japanese commander of the carrier task force missed a golden opportunity in restricting his attack on Pearl Harbor to one day's operations, and in the very limited choice of objectives.'

Navy Secretary Frank Knox was quickly on the scene to see for himself what had happened. That Sunday morning he had been closeted with Cordell Hull and Henry Stimson on the critical situation developing between his country and Japan, while two callers sat in an outer office waiting to see Cordell Hull – the one-eyed Ambassador Admiral Nomura and Japan's 'special envoy' Kurusu. When the conference ended Knox returned to his own office and had hardly settled into his chair before the Chief of Naval Operations, Admiral Harold R Stark, burst in on him with Ramsey's dramatic signal. Knox looked at it and said: 'My God, this can't be true! This must mean the Philippines!' 'No, sir,' said Admiral Stark, 'This is Pearl.'

It was about 1.45 pm and Knox put through an urgent call to Pearl Harbor. He then picked up the White House telephone and spoke to the President. 'I don't remember his exact words,' Knox recalled later. 'He was astonished, of course. I think he expressed disbelief . . .' When the President rang off Knox was connected to Pearl Harbor to speak to Rear-Admiral C C Bloch who gave him a concise account of the damage as it was then believed to be. Following this conversation Knox rushed to the White House for an extraordinary meeting of the President's Cabinet which had been called to discuss the war message the President was to deliver before Congress and to the American nation next day. 'I must know what happened at Pearl Harbor,' said Knox, 'I want all the details; I'm going out there.'

Meanwhile Nomura and Kurusu had reached the diplomatic waiting room outside Cordell Hull's office at 2.05 pm. Before they were admitted Roosevelt had spoken to Hull. 'Cordell,' he said sharply, 'Knox has just called with the report that the Japs have attacked Pearl Harbor.' 'Has it been confirmed?' Hull asked punctiliously. 'No, not yet,' the President replied, 'I have it only from Knox.' 'I'd like it confirmed before I see Nomura and Kurusu. They're outside in the waiting room,' Hull said.

At exactly 2.20 pm the two Japanese were admitted. They bowed and presented their note, Nomura explaining that he had had instructions to deliver it at one o'clock sharp and apologising that decoding difficulties had delayed them. Hull took the document from Nomura, adjusted his spectacles and began to read. (The contents were, of course known to him. But, as he said later he could give no indication that he knew what they were, and he had to make a pretence of reading the note.) It was the Japanese answer to Hull's memorandum of 26th November, a flat rejection of the US proposals and a farrago of self-justification and abuse. 'Ever since the China affair broke out,' it said, 'owing to the failure on the part of China to comprehend Japan's true intentions, the Japanese Government has striven for the restoration of peace . . . On the other hand, the American Government, always holding fast to theories in disregard of realities, and refusing to yield an inch on its impractical principles, caused undue delay in the negotiations . . . An attitude such as ignores realities and imposes one's selfish views on others will scarcely serv the purpose of facilitating the consummation of negotiations . . . Therefore . . . the Japanese Government regrets it cannot accept the proposal.' Cordell Hull's eyes blazed as he looked up at Japan's nervous envoys. 'In all my 50 years of public service,' he told them, 'I have never seen a document that was more crowded with infamous falsehoods and distortions – infamous falsehoods and distortions so huge that I never imagined until today that any Government on this planet was capable of uttering them.'

Nomura and Kurusu walked out, pale and quiet. Their job was done. They had carried out a useful delaying action which had helped to pave the way for the attack. They knew well enough that Japan was going to war with the United States, but to their deaths both maintained that they were ignorant of the details and did not know that Operation Z would reach its climax in the midst of their negotiations. But irrespective of whether Nomura and Kurusu had been unknowing or knowing agents of Japanese diplomacy the delay in delivering the note defeated the purpose its authors had designed for it. Emperor Hirohito did not get his wish, and what was universally regarded as a treacherous blow unified a badly divided and isolationist America. In assessing the relative cost to the Americans and the advantages gained by the Japanese from the Pearl Harbor operation it is probably this factor which counted most in the long run. Admiral Chuichi Hara, commander of the Japanese Fifth Carrier Division, *Shokaku* and *Zuikaku*, said wryly after the war: 'President Roosevelt should have pinned medals on us.'

For ten years, Japan had experienced nothing but victories over weak enemies, and the news of the attack astounded the Japanese people no less than it did the Americans. Excitement ran high when Imperial headquarters in Tokyo announced that the Japanese Army and Navy had 'entered into a state of war with American and British forces' and news flashes of the victory at Pearl Harbor, interspersed with the blare of patriotic marches, came over the radio. Crowds stood in the streets and sang the national anthem *Kimigayo;* thousands made their way to the plaza of the Imperial palace to bow and invoke the aid of the nation's divine ancestors. Newspaper boys ran through the streets sounding handbells and wooden clappers to announce special victory editions of the *Asahi*, the *Yomiuri* and *Nichi-nichi* dailies. 'Japan is NO Longer a Have-Not Country!' the headlines boasted. 'History is Now on the Side of the Axis . . . 100 Million are all Heroes'. 'The day for the march of our 100 million compatriots has come . . . The day we have been awaiting impatiently has arrived . . .' wrote the editor of the *Mainichi*, and undoubtedly the national mood was reflected by the editor of the *Nichi-nichi* when he said: 'Our Watchword today is "The Imperial Forces are invincible".'

From this beginning grew the malady of overconfidence which in Japan's dark years was aptly to be called the 'Victory Disease'. Conceit and arrogant underestimation of what they had taken on led eventually to the undoing of the Japanese. In the final analysis Japan's defeat can be traced back to this virus. Deep in the Japanese national character lies a streak of irrationality and impulsiveness combined with a strong sense of opportunism. Often indecisive and vacillating, the Japanese succumb readily to conceit, and the want of rationality often leads them to confuse desire and reality. This results in them doing things without proper consideration of the hazards; only when the result is failure do they think rationally about their actions, and then usually for the purpose of finding excuses for the failure. The tremendous gamble at Pearl Harbor paid off with the greatest victory the Japanese were fated to win. In December 1941, the rising sun of Japan had never shone more brilliantly. It did not start to set immediately, but that it should do so was inevitable. The long war which ensued was fought with all the skill and bravery and the senseless brutality which also goes to the make-up of the complex Japanese character. But never again would the Imperial Navy ever achieve the success which Fuchida's fliers brought it at Pearl Harbor.

Epilogue

The bombs that fell on Pearl Harbor were echoed by explosions in Hong Kong, in Thailand, and in Kota Bharu on the Thai-Malay border. In simultaneous attacks the Japanese struck at the perimeter of a vast arc extending from Hawaii to Thailand. At eight o'clock in the morning Honolulu time, Japanese task forces already deployed for action started to execute their separate blueprints of the master plan long prepared in Tokyo. According to General Tojo, Pearl Harbor was but an incident in a day from which all time would thereafter be calculated in *Dai Nippon*. But it was some eight hours after the attack before an Imperial rescript was published, officially declaring that Japan was engaged in the greatest gamble in his history: 'We, by the grace of Heaven, Emperor of Japan seated on the throne of a line unbroken for ages eternal, enjoin upon ye, our loyal and brave subjects;

We hereby declare war on the United States of America and the British Empire.

Men and officers of our Army and Navy shall do their utmost in prosecuting the war; . . . the entire nation with united will shall mobilise their total strength so that nothing will miscarry in the attainment of our war aims . . .

Eager for the realisation of their inordinate ambition to dominate the Orient, both America and Britain . . . have aggravated the disturbances in East Asia. Moreover, these two powers, inducing other countries to follow suit, increased military preparations on all sides of our Empire to challenge us. They have obstructed by every means our peaceful commerce, and finally have resorted to the direct severance of economic relations, menacing gravely the existence of our Empire . . .

The situation being such as it is, our Empire, for its existence and self-defence, has no other recourse but to appeal to arms and to crush every obstacle in its path . . .' These words did not necessarily represent Hirohito's own feelings any more than the Sovereign's Speech read at the opening of the British Parliament represents those of the British monarch. Nevertheless, included in this momen-

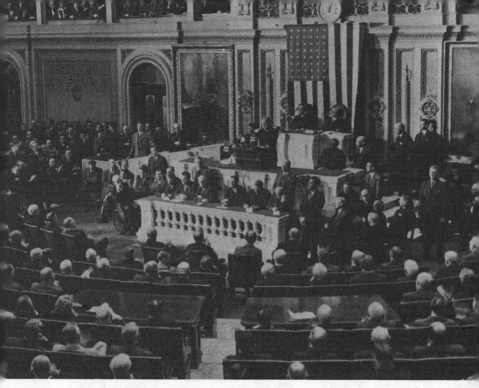

tous document there was one sentence which had been inserted at the Emperor's express wish: 'It has been truly unavoidable and far from our wishes that our Empire has now been brought to cross swords with America and Britain.'

In America, President Roosevelt, reporting to Congress next day, told of the 'unprovoked and dastardly attack' which had taken place on a day 'which will live in infamy'. It was a dishonourable deed and because of 'the distance of Hawaii from Japan . . . it is obvious that the attack was planned many days or even weeks ago. During the intervening time the Japanese Government has deliberately sought to deceive the United States by false statements and expressions of hope for continued peace.'

'Moreover,' the President continued grimly, 'the attack . . . has caused severe damage to American naval and military forces . . . very many American lives have been lost . . .' The President outlined the attacks which had immediately followed that on Pearl Harbor: Malaya, Hong Kong, Guam, the Philippines, Wake, Mid-

President Roosevelt addresses Congress on 8th December 1941

way. The Chamber was silent, until he said: 'Always will our whole nation remember the character of the onslaught against us.' At this there was an outburst of cheering. 'No matter how long it may take us to overcome this premediated invasion,' continued the President, 'the American people in their righteous might will win through to absolute victory. We will not only defend ourselves to the uttermost but will make it very certain that this form of treachery shall never endanger us again . . . We will gain the inevitable triumph – so help us God. I ask that the Congress declare . . . a state of war.'

In London, Winston Churchill addressed the House of Commons in a similar vein: 'Every circumstance of calculated and characteristic Japanese treachery was employed . . .' he declared. In Berlin Adolf Hitler told the Reichstag that a 'mentally insane' Roosevelt had provoked Japan into war. 'Germany's Asian ally,' he said 'has struck a blow at the American forger who had violated the rules of decency.' And in Rome, Benito Mussolini told a cheering crowd in the Plaza Venezia that 'the successful assault' in the Pacific had 'demonstrated the spirit of the soldiers of the Rising Sun' and that Italy was now united with 'heroic Japan'.

In Tokyo, Tojo broadcast to the Japanese nation shortly after the Imperial rescript had been published. Echoing the general theme of the royal edict, Japan's prime minister claimed that Japan had done her utmost to prevent war. Japan had never lost a war in 2,600 years, he said and 'I promise you final victory.' For some time the Japanese had been

aware that a crisis with America was fast approaching and after the initial shock they were wholeheartedly and enthusiastically in favour of the war. While the radio poured out bulletins which told of the irresistible progress of Japanese arms in south-east Asia, the newspapers gloated. Japan's future was assured, they said. The United States, claimed the *Japan Times*, reduced to a third-class naval power in a single morning, was now 'trembling in her shoes'. Pursuing the same theme a spokesman of the Naval General Staff predicted during a radio interview that 'Uncle Sam' would be forced to capitulate on the steps of the White House. Judging by the success of operations all over south-east Asia it seemed as if this might well be a valid possibility. Nothing, it appeared, could stop the warriors of the Rising Sun.

On 24th December, the first of Admiral Nagumo's ships arrived back

Below: Retribution . . . the aircraft-carrier *Hiryu* off Midway in June 1942, and the carrier *Ryukaku* after a successful US torpedo attack

at Japan after their triumphant twenty-nine-day operation. The carriers *Soryu* and *Hiryu* with the cruisers *Tone* and *Chikuma* and destroyers *Urikaze* and *Tanikaze* had broken off from the main force to support an invasion of Wake Island. Between 21st and 23rd December these ships made almost continuous strikes against Wake whilst the rest of the fleet steamed for home through heavy seas. (After fourteen days of unabated air and naval pounding the 400 strong garrison of US Marines was overwhelmed on 22nd December.) The *Akagi* and the *Kaga* arrived in Kure on Christmas Eve; next day they were joined by the *Shokaku* and *Zuikaku*, and three days later the *Hiryu* and *Soryu* sailed in from the Wake Island operation. Every ship received a tremendous ovation, and the airmen were lauded in the most lavish terms. Fuchida, especially, was the hero of the hour. Congratu-

lated, regaled and lionised, he was accorded the highest honour to which a Japanese could aspire when the Emperor expressed a desire to have a first hand report of the attack. Admiral Nagano, chief of the Naval General Staff, the man who had originally opposed Yamamoto's plan and who was now saying that it had been a 'splendid' operation, arranged the royal audience, and Nagumo, Fuchida and Shimazaki (who had led the second attack wave) were paraded at the Imperial palace. The audience, scheduled to last fifteen minutes, stretched out to forty-five. 'Were there any hospital ships in Pearl Harbor?' Hirohito asked Fuchida. 'And did you by chance hit such a ship?' 'No,' replied Fuchida nervously, speaking directly to the Emperor, and thereby creating a lapse of protocol. 'Were any civilian or unarmed training planes shot down?' enquired the Emperor anxiously. 'No,'

again replied Fuchida, falteringly. When the audience was over Fuchida said that the attack on Pearl Harbor had been less of an ordeal than telling the Emperor about it.

Throughout the fortnight of junketing and jubilation which followed the return of the fleet the silence of Admiral Yamamoto was noticeable. Although it was his victory which was being celebrated hysterically all over Japan, Yamamoto remained unmoved by the exuberant conviviality which surrounded him. His eyes were fixed warily on the future, and to his sister he wrote: 'Well, war has begun at last. But in spite of all the clamour that is going on we could lose it . . .' Despite a letter of congratulation from the Emperor (something which awed him) he remained uneasy. Before Pearl Harbor only a handful of American naval officers had ever heard of Isoruku Yamamoto. But after 7th December 1941 his name was on everyone's lips. To every American he became the embodiment of Japanese evil, the treacherous aggressor, the man who not only planned the Pearl Harbor attack, but who, in his arrogance, was also believed to be planning to dictate peace in the White House. He remained so until he was killed on Bougainville.

In his moment of glory Nagumo firmly rejected Yamamoto's criticisms that he had failed to inflict any damage on the American carriers or to have destroyed the oil storage tanks on Oahu. He had obeyed his orders to the letter, he maintained; he had destroyed the battleships and other military installations at Pearl Harbor. As for the American carriers, it was a pity that they were at sea when he attacked. But that was war. It was the answer of an unimaginitive leader. If Nagumo's carriers had sailed south to the Marshalls instead of returning by the northern route, his aircraft should have been able to locate the *Enterprise* and *Lexington*. The reason Nagumo gave for not doing so was that the fleet was short of fuel, and would miss the tankers, which were heading for a prearranged fuelling point on the northern route. Undoubtedly this decision was fortunate for the United States, for neither of the carriers would have been any match for the Japanese task force. Even if he had met *Enterprise* and *Lexington* together, Nagumo could have put 350 aircraft in the air against their 131. And with a superiority of nearly three to one there is little doubt that the American carriers would have been sunk.

If diplomatic problems and later strategic results are not considered, the attack on Pearl Harbor must be regarded as a short term operational masterpiece. But whether it was a long range mistake will be debated as long as naval history is written. With miniscule losses Japan inflicted tremendous damage on the US Pacific Fleet. As a result the Imperial Navy was able to race through the Pacific like a pack of killer whales. There was, however, an ironic element in the victory. The United States war plan, drawn up in contemplation of a conflict with Japan, called for the abandonment of the Philippines and other American outposts at the beginning of hostilities. It also called for a decisive battle with the Japanese fleet in the vicinity of the Marshalls or Western Carolines within six to nine months. Had Yamamoto been aware of this he would have realised that the attack on Pearl Harbor was not necessary. Where the Americans planned to give battle accorded with the traditional strategy for which the Combined Fleet had been training for over thirty years. The decision to attack Pearl Harbor was made only in the belief that the Pacific Fleet would move immediately to the Western Pacific to threaten Japan's operations in the south.

Whether or not the attack was a mistake in the long run and whether or not Nagumo failed to take every advantage, it was certainly a thoroughly planned and daring operation of rare precedence in history. Its originator knew the dangers full well and in a letter to a friend, written soon after the attack, he said: 'This war will give us much trouble in the future. The fact that we had a small success is nothing. The fact that we have succeeded so easily has pleased people. Personally I do not think it is a good thing to whip up propaganda to encourage the nation. People should think things over and realise how serious the situation is . . .'

In less than six months four of Yamamoto's precious carriers, *Akagi*, *Kaga*, *Soryu* and *Hiryu*, were at the bottom of the sea, casualties of the Battle of Midway. The tide of the Pacific war had turned, and in 1944, in Leyte Gulf, the Imperial Navy was reduced to a mere 'fish-pond fleet'. True to its traditions it fought magnificently but at the end of the battle it had virtually ceased to exist. By the end of the war Yamamoto's proud battleship, the *Nagato*, in which he had conceived the outlines of Operation Z, was a bombed-out hulk. Genda survived to become the Chief of Staff to a new Japanese air force, and a member of the Japanese parliament. Fuchida, severely wounded at Midway when the *Akagi* was sunk, also lived through the war to become a Protestant priest. But most of those who participated in the Pearl Harbor attack were destroyed in the holocaust it unleashed. Nagumo, whose decision to withdraw will long remain the subject of academic argument, committed *hari-kiri* on Saipan. In a hut which one of his staff set on fire, he shot himself; his body was never found. Yamamoto died honourably in combat while trying to restore confidence among the Japanese troops and boost their belief in ultimate victory. Early on 18th April 1943 he climbed into a camouflaged Japanese bomber at the air base at Rabaul and set off, accompanied by his staff in a second bomber, on a morale building tour of forward bases in the South Pacific. After the overwhelming defeat at Midway and the costly evacuation of Guadalcanal, the feeling of invincibility which had followed the attack on Pearl Harbor had been severely undermined, and Yamamoto's encouragement was badly needed.

But his mission had not gone unnoticed, and during the afternoon of 17th April an urgent signal had flashed from Washington to Guadalcanal. 'Washington Top Secret. Secret Navy to Fighter Control Henderson. Admiral Yamamoto, accompanied chief of staff and seven general officers Imperial Navy including surgeon grand fleet left Truk this morning . . .

Admiral and party travelling in two Betty [Japanese bombers] escorted six Zekes [fighters] . . . Itinerary: Arrive Rabaul 1630 hours where spend night. Leave dawn for Kahili where time of arrival 0945 hours . . . Squadron 339 P.38 must at all cost reach and destroy Yamamoto and staff morning April 18 . . . President attaches extreme importance this operation . . . [Signed] Frank Knox Secretary of State for Navy.' At the end of the message there was an addendum to the effect that this was an 'ultra-secret' document which must not be copied or filed.

That night, as American aircrews worked feverishly to prepare the aircraft for their mission of execution, a tropical rainstorm raged over Guadalcanal But the dawn of 18th April brought a clear blue sky, and soon after 7 am sixteen Lockheed Lightnings took off from the improvised strip, circled the palm-strewn island and then set course for Bougainville.

Sandwiched between six Japanese fighters Yamamoto's bombers were also flying towards Bougainville and by 9.30 am they had crossed the western coastline and were only a quarter of an hour away from their destination. Not until the pilots of the bombers saw four Lightnings streaking in towards them were they aware of approaching danger. But then the bombers dived towards the jungle and the Japanese Zekes turned to intercept the Americans. Too late. As Yamamoto's aircraft levelled out 200 feet above the treetops the four Lightnings had its rising sun emblem in their gun sights. The pilot twisted and swerved in vain; two short bursts of cannon fire and all was over. Trailing black smoke the bomber crashed into the trees and was quickly enveloped in flames. Yamamoto, the great strategist, was dead, and over 2,000 Americans killed at Pearl Harbor had been avenged. Perhaps he would not have wanted to survive in a Japan that suffered the humiliation of overwhelming defeat.

Pearl Harbor remains an imperative lesson in war, even in an age of nuclear power. Its lesson is one of history's bitter truths: that the unexpected can happen and often does.

Appendix A

CHRONOLOGY OF OPERATION Z
August 1939 Admiral Isoroku Yamamoto is appointed Commander-in-Chief of the Japanese Imperial Navy.
April/May 1940 The Japanese Combined Fleet holds manoeuvres, paying special attention to mock air attacks.
11th November 1940 In a daring night attack, aircraft of the Royal Navy sink three Italian battleships at their Taranto base in the Mediterranean.
December 1940 A suggestion that anti-torpedo nets should be erected in Pearl Harbor is rejected.
Admiral Yamamoto confides his ideas for an attack on Pearl Harbor to his chief of staff.
1941
27th January US Ambassador Joseph C Grew reports from Tokyo a rumour that Japan is planning a surprise attack on Pearl Harbor.
1st February Admiral Husband E Kimmel succeeds Admiral J O Richardson as Commander-in-Chief US Pacific Fleet. (Richardson was opposed to the Fleet being based at Pearl Harbor and had persistently urged its removal to the US West Coast.)
February/March In Tokyo, plans for Operation Z are drafted.
7th February General Walter C Short takes over as Commanding General, Hawaiian Command.
14th February President Roosevelt receives the new Japanese Ambassador, Admiral Kichisaburo Nomura.
8th March The United States passes the Lend-Lease Bill, authorising aid to any countries opposing members of the Tripartite Pact of September 1940 (Japan, Germany and Italy).
9th April Admiral Nomura presents the first of a succession of Japanese proposals for resolving US-Japanese difficulties. Further proposals are presented periodically up to 20th November 1941. Each of these proposals is unacceptable to the United States.

LANNED TIMINGS AND COORDINATION OF THE JAPANESE ATTACK N PEARL HARBOR

Resources

Aircraft available (Carrier-based)	**537**
Surface craft	**169**
Submarines	**64**

Timings

Time from decision to undertake Operation Z to first bomb drop	**35 days**
Time from departure of fleet to first bomb drop	**20 days**
Time from final decision to attack to first bomb drop	**24 hours**

Relative speeds

Aircraft	**150 – 250 knots**
Surface craft	**10 – 35 knots**
Submarines	**approximately 12 knots**

th April The United States begins Lend-Lease shipments to China.
th June The United States stops oil shipments from Atlantic and Gulf ports all countries except Britain and Latin America.
d July Japan calls up 1,000,000 men.
th July With the consent of the French Vichy government. Japanese troops cupy Southern Indo-China.
th July President Roosevelt freezes Japanese assets in the United States, oses all US ports to Japanese vessels and announces an embargo on the le of US petroleum products to Japan. (In consequence Japan must either cede to US demands for the withdrawal of her troops from China and do-China or seek alternative oil supplies. On 25th July Admiral Kimmel d General Short were told that sanctions would be imposed against Japan d that Japan was not expected to take any immediate hostile action.)
h August Admiral Nomura presents a Japanese proposal, in which Japan rees to make no advance beyond Indo-China and to evacuate Indo-China hen an agreement is reached with China, provided the United States will store free trade with Japan, discontinue aid to China, persuade China to gotiate a treaty favourable to Japan and recognise Japan's interests Indo-China.
h-12th August Churchill for Britain and Roosevelt for the United States ree on the principles of the Atlantic Charter.
th August In response to Prime Minister Konoye's proposal for a summit eeting between himself and President Roosevelt, the latter insists that reement on fundamental principles be reached at Ambassadorial level first.
h September The Japanese Imperial Conference decides on war if agreement ith the United States is not reached by early October.
th September The United States intercepts a message from Tokyo to the panese Consulate-General in Honolulu, ordering spies to report on S naval vessels in Pearl Harbor, according to a zoning grid stipulated the message.

9th October The United States deciphers the Pearl Harbor zoning intercept of 24th September. (For some months Washington has been able to decipher the Japanese Purple code, a secret diplomatic code, and other codes used to pass espionage directions. But often there is a delay of up to some weeks before such messages are deciphered and interpreted. The deciphered intercepts, given the name Magic, are distributed to a limited number of high-ranking US officials only.)

16th October Prime Minister Konoye is forced to resign. With the fall of Konoye's Cabinet, General Hideki Tojo becomes prime minister of Japan and forms a new Cabinet with Shigenori Togo as foreign minister.

16th October The US Chief of Naval Operations, Admiral Harold R Stark, warns Admiral Kimmel that Japanese aggression is a possibility.

3rd November Joseph C Grew, US ambassador in Tokyo, cables Washington that 'action by Japan which might render unavoidable an armed conflict with the United States may come with dangerous and dramatic suddenness'.

5th November Admiral Yamamoto issues Combined Fleet Top-Secret Order No 1, containing detailed plans for the attack on Pearl Harbor.

5th November The Japanese Privy Council authorises the submission of further proposals to the United States. By 20th November both plans have been rejected by the United States.

5th November The United States intercepts a message from Tokyo to Ambassador Nomura stating that the deadline for agreement with the US is 25th November.

15th November Special Envoy Saburo Kurusu arrives in Washington to assist Admiral Nomura in his negotiations with the US.

15th November The United States intercepts a message from Tokyo to the Japanese Consul-General in Honolulu, instructing his spies to make 'ships in harbour reports' irregularly, but twice a week.

17th November Ambassador Grew in Tokyo cables Washington a warning that Japan may strike suddenly and unexpectedly at any time.

20th November Ambassador Nomura and Special Envoy Kurusu present a 'final' Japanese proposal.

22nd November The United States intercepts a message from Tokyo to Nomura and Kurusu stating that the 25th November deadline is being extended until 29th November and that no further extension will be possible.

24th November The US Chief of Naval Operations warns Admiral Kimmel that a Japanese 'surprise aggressive movement' is a possibility.

26th November The Pearl Harbor task force, under command of Admiral Nagumo sails from Tankan Bay in the Kuriles, destined for a point about 200 miles north of Oahu.

26th November US Secretary of State, Cordell Hull, hands to Nomura and Kurusu the US reply to the Japanese Note of 20th November.

27th November The US Chief of Naval Operations, and the US Army Chief of Staff separately notify Admiral Kimmel and General Short that diplomatic negotiations with the Japanese have collapsed and that Japanese aggression may be expected. (In three messages between 27th and 28th November the War Department warned Hawaii specifically against sabotage.)

27th November The US Chief of Naval Operations suggests that Admiral Kimmel should arrange to deliver twenty-five aircraft each to Wake Island and Midway, as soon as possible.

27th November Tokyo tells Nomura and Kurusu that although a rupture in their negotiations with the US is now inevitable they are not 'to give the impression that negotiations are broken off'.

28th November Admiral Kimmel orders that submerged submarines in the vicinity of Pearl Harbor are to be regarded as hostile.

29th November The United States intercepts a message from Tokyo to the Japanese Consulate-General in Hawaii telling his agents to report the *absence* of ship movements at Pearl Harbor.

30th November The Japanese Cabinet approves the text of a '14-Part' Note

hich is to be sent in answer to Cordell Hull's proposal of 26th November.
mperor Hirohito insists that the Note should be submitted before
ostilities begin.

t December The Japanese Privy Council, meeting in the presence of the
mperor, authorises an attack on Pearl Harbor.

id December The United States intercepts a message from Tokyo to the
apanese Embassy at Washington, instructing the Ambassador to destroy
is codes.

h December The United States intercepts a message to Tokyo from Japanese
gents in Honolulu saying 'there is considerable opportunity left to take
lvantage for a surprise attack against these places'. A second message
ates that 'it appears that no air reconnaissance is being conducted
y the fleet air arm'. (This message was not deciphered until 8th December.)

h December By about 9.30 am President Roosevelt has read a deciphered
ersion of most of the '14-Part' Note, which the Japanese ambassador has
een told not to deliver until a time which will be expressly stipulated
y Tokyo.

h December 9.20 am (Washington time; 3.50 am Honolulu time).
he minesweeper USS *Condor* sights a submarine periscope outside the
atrance to Pearl Harbor.

h December About eleven o'clock (Washington time; 5.30 am Honolulu time)
1e US Chief of Staff and Chief of Naval Operations receive a deciphered copy
' the final part of the Japanese '14-Part' Note, and a message from Tokyo
▶ the effect that the Note should be delivered at one o'clock in the afternoon
Washington time; 7.30 am Honolulu time). At 12.18 pm (Washington time;
18 am Honolulu time), the Chief of Staff cables General Short (with copy
▶ Admiral Kimmel) telling him of the time specified for delivery of the
1-Part' Note. This warning does not reach either General Short or
dmiral Kimmel until after the attack.

h December 12.15 pm (Washington time; 6.45 am Honolulu time)
1e destroyer USS *Ward* sinks a submarine outside the Pearl Harbor boom.

h December 1.25 pm – 1.55 pm (Washington time; 7.55 am – 8.25 am
onolulu time) Japanese aircraft attack United States warships in
earl Harbor, and airfields on Oahu where aircraft are lined up wing-tip to
ing-tip for anti-sabotage defence.

h December 1.55 pm approximately (Washington time; 8.25 am
onolulu time) a second wave of Japanese aircraft attack Oahu.

h December 3.15 pm (Washington time; 9.45 am Honolulu time)
1e Japanese aircraft retire.

h December The Japanese launch attacks on the Philippines, Hong Kong
1d Malaya.

h December Four o'clock (Washington time; 10.30 am Honolulu time).
n Imperial Rescript, signed by Emperor Hirohito, declaring war on the
nited States and Britain, is issued.

h December The United States Congress passes a resolution declaring
ar on Japan.

h December Britain declares war on Japan.

h December Secretary of the Navy Frank Knox leaves the US for Hawaii
▶ assess the damage at Pearl Harbor.

'th December In accordance with the terms of the Tripartite Treaty,
ermany and Italy declare war on the United States and the United States
eclares war on Germany and Italy.

'th-26th December The Japanese Pearl Harbor task force arrives back in Japan.

Appendix B

SUMMARY OF THE PEARL HARBOR LOSSES
In December 1941 the US Pacific Fleet included twelve capital ships:
nine battleships and three aircraft carriers. Of these, eight battleships but
none of the carriers were in Pearl Harbor on the morning of 7th December.
(The battleship *Colorado* was in the Bremerton Navy Yard; the carrier
Enterprise was on its way back to Pearl Harbor from Wake; the *Lexington*
was ferrying aircraft to Midway; the *Saratoga* was undergoing repairs on the
West Coast of the United States.)

RESULTS OF THE ATTACK
Eighteen ships sunk or seriously damaged out of a total of about
ninety-six in Pearl Harbor at the time of the attack.

Battleships:
Arizona, total loss, when her forward magazine blew up;
Oklahoma, total loss, capsised and sunk in harbour. (Later she was raised
solely to clear harbour of the obstruction and resunk off Oahu);
California and *West Virginia*, sunk at their berths with quarterdecks awash.
(Later they were raised and repaired);
Nevada, beached while under way out of the harbour to prevent sinking
in deep water. (Later repaired);
Pennsylvania, *Maryland* and *Tennessee*, all received damage but of a less
severe character.

Target ship:
Utah (former battleship) sunk.

Smaller ships
Cruisers: *Helena*, *Honolulu* and *Raleigh* were all damaged, but were
eventually repaired.
Destroyers: Two (*Cassin* and *Downes*) damaged beyond repair;

JAPANESE TARGETS ON THE MORNING OF 8th DECEMBER 1941
(JAPANESE TIME)

Location	Number	Description
Pearl Harbor	6	Attack from the air in two waves
Philippines	10	4 targets for aerial attack (two waves for 2 targets); 6 landings (only five of which were carried out)
Malaya	9	5 targets for aerial attack; 3 landings and an inland incursion from Thailand
Thailand	1	Army march across border and seize Bangkok
Guam	1	Air attacks followed by assault landings
Wake	1	Air attacks followed by assault landings
Hong Kong	1	Air attacks followed by assault landings

two others damaged but repaired later.
Minelayer: *Ogala*, sunk but salvaged later.
Auxiliary vessels: Seaplane tender *(Curtiss)* and repair ship *(Vestal)* were both severely damaged but repaired later.

Aircraft:
A total of 188 US aircraft destroyed. (Ninety-two aircraft of the US Navy and ninety-six of the US Army Air Force). An additional 128 Army and thirty-one Navy aircraft were damaged. Kaneohe and Ewa airfields suffered most. Of the eighty-two aircraft on these two fields only one was airworthy after the attack.

Casualties:
Navy: 2,008 officers and enlisted men killed; 710 wounded.
Marines: 109 officers and enlisted men killed; sixty-nine wounded.
Army: 218 officers and enlisted men killed; 364 wounded.
Civilians: Sixty-eight killed, thirty-five wounded.
Total Casualties: 2,403 killed, 1,178 wounded.
Of the 2,403 killed nearly half were lost when the *Arizona* blew up.

Other Damage:
During the attack bombs and US anti-aircraft fire caused damage in the city of Honolulu. The extent of this damage was assessed at 500,000 dollars.

JAPANESE LOSSES:
Twenty-nine aircraft (nine fighters, fifteen dive bombers and five torpedo-bombers did not return from the attack.)
In addition the submarine advance expeditionary force lost one I-class submarine and all five midgets.
Total personnel lost: 185 (this figure includes the nine crew of the midget submarines and fifty-five airmen.)

Bibliography

The Chrysanthemum and the Sword Ruth Benedict (Houghton Mifflin, Boston)
Tojo: The Last Banzai Courtney Browne (Angus & Robertson, London)
Tojo and the Coming of the War Robert J C Butow (Princeton University Press Princeton)
The Broken Seal Ladislas Farago (Random House, New York)
The Road to Pearl Harbor Herbert Feis (Princeton University Press, Princeton)
Midway Mitsuo Fuchida and Masatake Okumiya (US Naval Institute Annapolis, Maryland)
Ten Years in Japan Joseph C Grew (Simon and Schuster, New York)
Turbulent Era Joseph C Grew (Houghton Mifflin, Boston)
Red Sun Rising: The Siege of Port Arthur Reginald Hargreaves (Weidenfeld and Nicolson, London. J B Lippincott, Philadelphia)
The Divine Wind Inoguchi, Rikihei, Nakajima, Tadashi and Roger Pineau (Hutchinson, London)
The End of the Imperial Navy Masanori Ito (Weidenfeld and Nicolson, London)
The Rise and Fall of the Japanese Empire David H James (Allen and Unwin, London)
The War Against Japan Volume I S Woodburn Kirby (HMSO, London)
Day of Infamy Walter Lord (Holt, Rinehart, and Winston, New York)
Hirohito: Emperor of Japan Leonard Mosley (Weidenfeld and Nicolson, London. Prentice-Hall, New York)
Admiral of the Pacific John Deane Potter (Heinemann, London)
The Double Patriots Richard Storry (Chatto and Windus, London. Houghton Mifflin, Boston)
A History of Modern Japan Richard Storry (Penguin Books, London)
Pearl Harbor: Warning and Decision Roberta Wohlstetter (Stanford University Press, Stanford)